STEVEN GERRARD

My Liverpool Story

With Paul Joyce

headline

First published in 2012 by Headline Publishing Group

3

Cataloguing in Publication Data is available from the British Library

Hardback ISBN 978 0 7553 6394 0
Ebook ISBN 978 0 7553 6397 1

Typeset in Avant Garde Gothic and Lubalin Graph

Design and art direction by James Edgar at Post98design.co.uk

Printed in Great Britain by Butler Tanner & Dennis Ltd, Frome and London.

Headline's policy is to use papers that are natural, renewable and recyclable products and made from wood grown in sustainable forests. The logging and manufacturing processes are expected to conform to the environmental regulations of the country of origin.

Headline Publishing Group
An Hachette UK Company
338 Euston Road
London NW1 3BH

www.headline.co.uk
www.hachette.co.uk

DEDICATION

I would like to dedicate this book to my family, especially my wife, Alex, and my three beautiful daughters, Lilly-Ella, Lexie and Lourdes.

I hope that, by reading it, they better understand my story and can learn from my experiences, both good and bad, in a game I love.

ACKNOWLEDGEMENTS

I would like to thank Struan Marshall and Kathryn Taylor at Wasserman and Andy Sterling of Benson McGarvey for their advice and help throughout my career. Thanks also to Jonathan Taylor and Richard Roper of Headline Publishing Group for their expertise in putting the book together, Paul Joyce of the *Daily Express* for helping to get my thoughts down and to Ged Rea and Dave Ball for collating all the statistics.

CONTENTS

FOREWORD

Football players are forever finding themselves pigeon-holed. You hear claims all the time that so and so is the best at this, someone else is the best at that, or no one has ever done this quite as well before. In the end, I am not sure any of it really matters. It is down to personal preference most of the time, anyway.

But when I think about Steven Gerrard and Liverpool, one fact is indisputable: the enormous contribution Steven has made to the history of the football club from the moment he first stepped out on the turf wearing that red shirt.

People should just be grateful that they have had the opportunity to watch Steven grow as a player, and as a person, before their very eyes, and take heart from the reality that he has brought so much excitement and joy to everyone in the process.

I have admired Steven from afar as a fantastic midfielder who leads by example on the pitch, but also off it with the way he conducts himself and speaks so honestly and passionately about Liverpool, and I count myself lucky to have worked closely alongside him, day in, day out, when I returned to Anfield as manager.

It was disappointing that I couldn't select him as often as I would have liked due to injury in that period, but I know exactly what Steven went through for Liverpool Football Club during my time back at the helm, especially the lengths he went to in order to make himself available for selection.

I am not being disrespectful to any of the other players, but when Steven trained with the squad the quality in the sessions simply went up another notch – firstly because he is such a good player, but also because his team-mates sensed that quality amongst them and knew they had to raise their own games to try and match his. That tells you something about his presence and also the respect he receives as a colleague and a captain.

When I think about Steven Gerrard and Liverpool, I consider theirs to be the perfect fit. On the one hand you have a marvellous player who is living out his dreams with his boyhood favourites and, on the other, you have a magnificent club that has helped him to fulfil most of his ambitions.

Theirs is a relationship that has suited both parties. A match made on Merseyside.

Kenny Dalglish, August 2012

INTRODUCTION

Every year, I am presented with countless
opportunities to do books about my career. I usually
turn them down flat. However, the chance to tell
'My Liverpool Story' through my words and the
photographs which frame my life was too good
a chance to overlook.

Sifting through all the pictures stirred great
memories and I hope those who read this book gain
the same level of enjoyment I have had in writing it.
Each day I realise how lucky I am to live the dream.

Hopefully, there are a few more chapters still to
be written in my time at Anfield, a few more trophies
to lift and a few more highs to sample.

Steven Gerrard, August 2012

CHAPTER 1

1980 — 1998

THREE WORDS CHANGED MY LIFE: LIVERPOOL WANT YOU

I didn't realise it at the time, but when my dad told me of the interest from Anfield one night at home in Huyton everything altered for me: my direction in life, the path I'd take growing up, the choices I'd make from that day on.

I was just a baby – eight years old – but that was that. A full-blown love affair had been ignited.

Dave Shannon, a coach at Liverpool's Centre of Excellence, had approached Ben McIntyre, the manager of my local Sunday League team, Whiston Juniors, and he then relayed the news to my dad.

My dad wasn't really surprised. He had grown used to scouts pulling him to one side after games. 'Is the midfielder your lad?' they would ask. 'We like him. We would like him to come and train with us.'

Manchester United, Everton and Manchester City had all been in touch and basically Liverpool's interest snowballed from there. They didn't want one of their deadly rivals pinching a talent from under their noses and so invited me to go for a trial in the old Vernon Sangster Sports Centre that used to be in the shadow of Anfield, but is now no longer there, or to Melwood in the school holidays.

Melwood? The place where Liverpool's first team train? Me?

Just to be driven through the iron gates of the training ground was an amazing feeling and on the way there with my dad I was imagining bumping into the likes of John Barnes and Ronnie Whelan.

Of course, there was no chance of that. The first team had long since gone home and it was night before the kids were allowed in. As it was, the first thing that really struck me about being in this magical, hallowed place that had been graced by some of the greatest players ever to play football was ... the grass. It wasn't like the scrap of land where I pretended to be a professional footballer every spare minute I had growing up in Ironside Road. It was like a carpet, a bowling green. Perfect.

At that age, I didn't have a clue if I was good or not. Whiston Juniors was a well-run club and used to produce a programme with match reports in them. I was scoring hat-tricks, getting Man of the Match and we were beating teams heavily, every week.

I knew I was important for my Sunday League side, maybe the best in the league, but when you turn up at Liverpool to play in a small trial game and see other young lads doing the turns and flicks that you've been practising it was like: wow! There are other good players out there too! A whole new world opened up in front of me and it was one I was desperate to be a part of.

Back then, at the very start of my career, I was more scared and nervous than anything else. I didn't know what to expect, what Liverpool wanted from me. But I was soon put at ease.

The first three people I met were the coaches Steve Heighway, Hughie McAuley and Dave, who had started the whole process off. From day one until the day I turned professional, they were there for me. And they would still be there for me if I needed anything.

They were a team and all used to sing off the same hymn sheet. They believed in the same values of the club and looking back on it now they became like uncles to me. I felt as though I was part of a family because they treated me that well.

Don't get me wrong, there were times when they could give out a telling off – Steve would normally be the one to do that – but they always wanted the best for me.

Liverpool's support didn't stop me from trying out different clubs. Going elsewhere allowed me to see what those clubs were like compared to Liverpool, but I never got the same feeling.

I went to Manchester United on a five-day trial during the school holidays and I met Sir Alex Ferguson. I went to West Ham and scored a couple of goals in a trial game against Cambridge, which we won 6-2.

I spent four days with West Ham when I was 11 and at the end of it they offered me a three-year professional contract for when I was 17. Maybe I was better than I thought after all. Everton were also keen on offering me a deal around the same time, but they never had a chance. They were pestering my dad all the time to get me to go in and have a look around

> **Melwood? The place where Liverpool's first team train? Me?**

and play in a game for them and eventually I did just that, to ensure my dad got a break from them as much as anything. I started a game for them, but at half-time I was taken off. To this day I don't know why. Maybe they had seen enough, but there were a lot of kids there that day so they could have wanted to give someone else a chance. But I took it as an insult. Everton had been asking me to go there for months and months and months and then they dragged me off. I just thought if I am going to impress you, I want a full match to do it in.

There were also a couple of games for Tranmere as a favour to one of my dad's mates. I was never going to go there, but I did follow them a bit. Ged Brannan was from the same estate as me and he played for them and used to get us tickets every now and then, so I did have a bit of a soft spot for them.

Really though, I wanted to play for Liverpool. My team. And Liverpool wanted me.

Steve Heighway was happy for me to go and try other places, test the water, but he'd always have a message for Dad before I went anywhere. 'Don't do anything stupid because we want Steven,' he'd say. 'And we want him for a long time.'

DREAMING OF ANFIELD

I trained at Liverpool a couple of times a week when I was first starting out. It was the club I supported, but I didn't appreciate what Liverpool meant back then. I didn't understand how big the club was, how it had thousands of people in the city under its spell, and millions more across the world, and I probably didn't understand how lucky I was.

I was just bothered about football and at that stage it didn't matter who it was for. Whether it was for Liverpool, my school, Cardinal Heenan School, or Whiston Juniors didn't bother me at that time. I just wanted to play.

Every day I practised in the street. While I was waiting for my dad to take me to Melwood, I'd be juggling a ball by the car. If we were getting the bus, I'd dribble the ball to the stop. Every morning I'd check my school bag to make sure I hadn't forgotten anything that I would need that day. Making sure I had a ball for break, lunchtime and after school, was my first priority and after that my books.

I did dream about Liverpool though. A lot. From being the eight-year-old who didn't know how good he was, I remember the first time I started to think I might have a chance of making it was when Michael Owen and me were asked to go with Liverpool U18s for a tournament in Spain. We were 11 at the time. From the first moment I saw Michael in those early games at the Vernon Sangster, I knew he was brilliant. He scored for fun when we were kids. Ice cold in front of goal even at that age.

There were between 10 and 14 players in our age group at Liverpool, but only Michael and I were invited to San Sebastian. We didn't play, it was just for experience, but privately I figured that for us to be the only ones invited meant the coaches thought we had a good chance. I don't know whether they rated me as highly as Michael, but just being on that trip to sunny Spain helped me focus.

With progress comes responsibility. I wasn't really one for school, I didn't like doing homework for starters, but there was no way that my dad would allow me to misbehave. It was about respect. There were times when I would get above my station with the PE teachers and try and act the big shot because I was training at

Liverpool, but if they had ever told my dad he would have come down heavy on me.

Liverpool stressed, too, that the invites to Melwood would stop for anyone going off the rails at school and causing trouble. I didn't fancy testing things to see if Steve Heighway was making an empty threat or a promise.

At the age of 14, another mini-milestone arrived. Liverpool offered me two years' schoolboy forms, an apprenticeship and then a three-year professional contract when I turned 17. They did rate me, and highly.

While most of my mates at school had trouble scraping together a few quid, I had it written down in black and white on Liverpool-headed notepaper in a draw in my house how much I would be earning until I was 20. When I turned professional, I would be on £700-a-week rather than a month. The next year £800-a-week and then £900-a-week.

The sums were mind-boggling really. My life was being mapped out in front of me, but it was never, ever about money for me. It was just about football.

I think everyone who is at a Centre of Excellence or on schoolboy forms believes they will make it. At the end of the day, you are at Liverpool for a reason. But there were times when I realised it wasn't going to be all plain sailing, which is a route that my career has followed ever since. Every time I would step up in an age group, it dawned on me just how hard it was going to be to eventually pull on the red shirt. I was still tiny and everyone else was stronger, bigger and faster than me. In those circumstances, I am sure there have been good players who have slipped through the net and not been given the opportunity to fulfil their potential. There was no way that was going to happen to me and, fortunately, I was able to make up for those disadvantages in other areas. Team-mates and rivals used to tower over me, but football-wise I was head and shoulders above them. I saw things differently on the pitch, spotted the pass quicker than many of them and then delivered it better.

There was a game at Melwood when I was in the final year of secondary school and Liverpool had asked me to play for the B-team. I ended up being substitute for the A-team, however, and came on in the final 20 minutes of a match against Blackburn. I did well, won tackles, sprayed some passes around, and as I walked off afterwards I heard a voice next to me: 'You'll walk into Liverpool's first team.' It was Jamie Redknapp. He had been watching the game and pulled me aside after the final whistle. That was a huge moment for me. Jamie wasn't just a member of the first team, he was my hero. He was the boy back then. The one I looked up to probably because I played in the same position as him – central midfield – and he had everything I wanted.

'Thanks,' I said nervously. I didn't say much else. I was in awe.

Afterwards, I was walking on air. I rushed home to tell my mum and dad and brother, Paul, but no one else. I kept things to myself in lots of ways and those who didn't need to know didn't find out. Many people said I was good at that stage of my career, but this was Jamie Redknapp. England's Jamie Redknapp. He knew his football and I thought to myself he's not going to waste his words on someone he doesn't think merits them, he obviously believed it. It was the first time I had any real contact with Jamie, but he was hugely important to me in those early years at Liverpool. If I needed advice he was there for me and he still is.

Going full-time as a professional is one of the greatest feelings I have had in football, besides the medals I've won and the big nights I've enjoyed, but the best days of my career were when I was an apprentice without a shadow of doubt.

I had my own standards and wanted to play well every week just like now, but there wasn't the pressure. At that stage there aren't a dozen newspapers pouring over your performances, half-a-dozen TV channels dissecting whether you have played well or not, or loads of magazines predicting how you will do. You basically had Steve Heighway, Hughie McAuley and Dave Shannon guiding you, and 30 of your mates with you every day. For two years, we had a laugh and

> **"**
> **Every time I would step up in an age group, it dawned on me just how hard it was going to be to eventually pull on the red shirt.**
> **"**

played on brilliant football pitches. We were all together and we were changing from boys into men. Passing our driving tests together, getting cars (I used to drive my mum's Nissan Bluebird before splashing out on an N-reg red Golf) and lending each other fivers and tenners. I can remember putting a few extra miles on my expenses to try and squeeze some extra pounds out of Steve Heighway.

Initially, there wasn't the same pressure for me because I had the promise of turning professional, but that soon changed. Michael Owen changed everything for me. As soon as he went full-time, he was away. Playing for the reserves, scoring the goals that helped Liverpool win the FA Youth Cup in 1996 against a West Ham team containing Rio Ferdinand and Frank Lampard, and then into the first team.

That was when I felt the pressure creeping in – and jealousy, too, because I wanted to get to where he was as quickly as he had done it. His status changed. I wasn't just going to watch Redknapp, Fowler and McManaman at Anfield any more. I was watching them and Michael and Jamie Carragher, too, who I had been sharing a dressing room with only a few months earlier. A bit of frustration crept into me as a footballer for the first time because I wanted it to happen as quickly for me as it had for Michael. Physically, he was ready. I wasn't and had to be more patient.

But Michael was certainly a big influence in terms of driving me forward. Seeing what he was doing, the highs he was enjoying, gave me the incentive to push on.

CHAPTER 2

1998
—
1999

NOVEMBER 29, 1998

I can remember every minute and every hour as if it was yesterday. Arriving at the ground, getting changed, warming up and then standing on the touchline, nervous as hell, waiting to come on for my Liverpool debut at Anfield against Blackburn Rovers.

The fourth official held up Vegard Heggem's number and I bounded on for the final three minutes, including injury time, of a 2-0 win that had earlier been sealed by goals from Paul Ince and Michael Owen.

This was it, everything I had dreamed about. There was a huge adrenaline buzz. Being clapped on by thousands of people, creating a wall of noise, sends a tingle through your body, but the biggest emotion I felt was relief. I was playing for Liverpool's first team. No one could take that away from me now. I had realised a dream. My dad said as much to me on the way home afterwards and then paused before adding: 'But that has to be the start. You've done nothing. Don't rest on that.'

It was good advice, but I knew myself I wanted to taste more. It was another life-changing experience. This wasn't playing in front of 200 people for the reserves. There was a crowd of almost 42,000 inside Anfield and, for a moment, as I prepared to come on their focus was drawn to me. To be honest, most of the supporters probably thought: 'Who's this skinny little lad?' I had only played four games for the reserves. Our FA Youth Cup team was knocked out of that competition in the early rounds, so it wasn't like it had been with Michael who everyone sat up and took notice of straight away.

People thought I might have been a decent player, but that was as far as it went. Looking back that helped me in some respects. The youngsters at Liverpool don't have that luxury now. The U18s' and reserves' matches are all live on the club's TV channel, LFC TV, and that

can be counterproductive. Look at someone like Raheem Sterling. He has got a big reputation for himself because everyone has seen him terrorising defences on the club channel. There is an expectation that comes with that which makes life difficult. Thankfully from what I see of Raheem, I think he is someone who is taking it all in his stride and he has a good chance of forging a successful career for himself in red. He is a level-headed kid and I see similarities with how I was at 17. Raheem is quiet, but he comes alive in training and on the pitch.

For me, those very first sessions I had with the first team were so important not only in my development, but in also ensuring I was accepted by players I had previously idolised. Liverpool's academy was just getting up and running in Kirkby, but Gerard Houllier, the Liverpool manager, called up myself and Stephen Wright to Melwood rather than letting us go there. Immediately my progress snowballed.

I knew I had to make an impression. If I trained well, I knew people would sit up and take notice of me. I made it my mission, from the very first session in which I was involved, to catch the eye.

But it was intimidating at the same time. Ince, Berger, Redknapp, Fowler, McManaman, Babb and Staunton were not just Liverpool players but proven internationals as well. I was scared to talk to them and terrified to give the ball away. From the moment I started training with Liverpool, there was another change I had to get used to.

I may have been 18, but those players don't see a young lad standing before them. If I was good enough to be their team mate, then I was good enough to be judged as an equal. It was sink or swim. Give the ball away and you get told about it. Paul Ince wasn't going to cut me any slack. That was clear when I made my full debut against Tottenham, the weekend after my cameo against Blackburn. I was playing out of position at right-back and found myself up against David Ginola, one of the best players in the Premier League, but that didn't matter to Incey. He was on my back for the majority of the 57 minutes I was on the pitch. Where Robbie Fowler was really supportive, Incey was shouting at me, telling me to sort myself out and keep track of the French winger who was giving me the run around.

We lost 2-1. I was dragged off so I didn't need telling that my full debut had not been a success. I hated Incey after that game. I had endured bad games growing up, but nothing like this. I doubted myself and was concerned that my Liverpool career would be over almost before it had begun.

Obviously, I was worrying too much, but at the time you just hope the next game will be easier. You don't think, 'I'll learn from being ripped apart by David Ginola at White Hart Lane.' Nowadays I would prefer to receive the treatment Incey gave me that day. Yes, I felt sorry for myself and sulked at the time, but he wasn't picking on me for the sake of it. He was pushing me to become the best I could be.

I was fortunate that Liverpool played Celta Vigo in the UEFA Cup just three days after my Tottenham ordeal. It was my third game for the club and I knew how important it was. Thankfully, I was back in midfield, my position, and I did well. I felt comfortable straight away: finding my passing range, making tackles and redressing the balance from the previous game against Spurs.

> **"**
> **I was playing for Liverpool's first team. No one could take that away from me now.**
> **"**

We lost 1-0, but looking back on that match I believe it was a key one for me because it gave Houllier the confidence to persist with me. If I had bombed in that game as well, he might have decided it was better to take me out of the front line. Instead, he stuck by me and I was given another chance to prove myself when we played Everton in the April of that season. It was my first taste of a Merseyside derby and I wasn't about to let the Bluenoses ruin my weekend. It was 71 minutes before I came on, once again for Heggem, but I made my mark. I threw myself into tackles, almost ripping the shirt off Danny Cadamateri's back at one point before kicking an effort from him off the line with the goal gaping, as Everton sought to make it 3-3 in a pulsating game.

Anfield exploded as we kept our slender advantage intact and I even celebrated stopping the equaliser, shaking my fists before getting pats on the back from my team-mates. It felt like I was the match-winner. There is no better way to win supporters round than ensuring they had the bragging rights in a derby. Now the fans could put their trust in me. I was one of them. I had only been on the pitch for 19 minutes, but I crammed so much into that time that as I headed back to the dressing room after the final whistle it felt like I was floating on air.

The next time I faced Everton, however, I was to trudge from the pitch with very different emotions.

Starting to Contribute

In the few minutes I played on my debut, I had five or six touches. There were a couple of short passes, I took a throw-in and I over-hit two crosses. You do worry when you are just a kid and the cross you've put into the penalty box sails over the intended target. If I over-hit a cross now, people will expect the next one to be good.

Back then, the fans didn't know anything about me and I was desperate to make a good impression. Without being big-headed, the shape and technique I am using in the picture shows how to whip the ball over with pace. You practise crossing like all other aspects of your game. A lot of players find it hard to get that shape.

Gerard Houllier – The Master

I love seeing pictures of Gerard, and I love meeting him at games. I still have a lot of contact with him. There will be phone calls and texts from him before a big game and he is still encouraging me and giving me advice.

I will always listen to what Gerard Houllier has to say and that illustrates the respect I have for him. He is someone who I owe an awful lot of gratitude to because without him I would not have had the career I have had.

Pushing Me to Be the Best

Paul Ince was one of my heroes when I was watching England as a kid and so when he signed for Liverpool I was delighted. This was a chance for me to learn from one of the best around. But when I got to a certain age, Incey became an 'enemy' (in a good way you understand) for me because I knew I had to try and push him for his place in the team. Yes he was a hero, but he was also standing in my way of a regular place in Liverpool's starting line-up. He used to get on my back an awful lot when I first started playing in the team and that can be hard to take when you are tentatively feeling your way into the team. 'What was that?' he would bark at me, or 'Stop giving the ball away' – I've taken out the swear words in between! Deep down I knew Incey had my best interests at heart, however, and it was his way of pushing me. He was doing it for the right reasons and that is why, to this day, I have an awful lot of time for him as a player and a person.

First Taste of Europe

An aerial duel in my first European start against Celta Vigo at Anfield, although I can't have got up very high if David Thompson is level with me! My first action in a Liverpool shirt against Blackburn and Tottenham had come out of position and as a result I felt out of my depth a bit. Here, I was in central midfield and in the thick of the action.

I loved it. This was my position and I started the game well which gave me a huge boost to my confidence. The UEFA Cup was important in my development because I learnt about different styles and got to experience different types of football. In the background is Michel Salgado, ex-Real Madrid, Spain and also Blackburn.

In Awe of 'God'

Liverpool used to get me match tickets when I was young, but on the occasions I felt too ashamed to ask for them I would pay to go to the game and stand on the Kop. Robbie Fowler was my first idol. He was the man on fire, banging goals in left, right and centre. He was one of the best finishers in the world.

It was surreal for me when I later became his team-mate. I was in awe to begin with, but Robbie was one of the players who helped me the most. He'd offer little tips, but mainly he made sure I was always involved in whatever was happening. He has always been there for me and I am good friends with him now.

CHAPTER 3

1999
2000

SEEING RED

When I was younger I could be a nasty piece of work on the pitch. Off it I was quite shy. On it, I became someone else. Someone I didn't like. I am not proud of that. In fact, I am embarrassed when I think back to how I used to be and how I used to act when I stepped onto a football pitch. Too often in my younger days, around the time I was 14, I crossed the line. Away from football, I was well-behaved: mischievous at times like all teenage schoolboys, but nothing more sinister. Put a pair of boots on me and a kit and there was a time when I didn't know whether I would score a goal, and be named Man of the Match, or get sent off. I was a liability.

I didn't go out to try and deliberately hurt opponents, but it was just a case of wanting to be a success so much that my temperament boiled over at times.

The staff at Liverpool recognised early in my development that this side of my game needed to be smoothed out. My aggressive approach became an issue because there were occasions when I had fall-outs with Hughie McAuley, and later on Sammy Lee, in training. They were just trying to help me, but sometimes you don't want, or don't feel you have, to listen.

It wasn't just Steve Heighway, Dave Shannon and Hughie who recognised this.

Ronnie Moran and Roy Evans, the coaches with the first team, did their best to try and calm me down and ensure I could channel my talents more efficiently.

They had seen some of the tackles I'd made for the reserves in A and B games. It was as if that particular match was the most important in the world to me and no one was going to get in my way.

My dad was called in to a meeting with the coaches at Melwood one night and I was left to wait at home for the verdict. When he arrived back, he was blunt. 'You need to sort yourself out or you'll get nowhere,' he said. He was speaking for my own sake, to try and prevent me from getting seriously injured, and for the safety of other people.

No one at Liverpool wanted to take the hunger out of my game. They said I had a fantastic chance of making it because of my will to win, but I was overly keen. It was something I had to work on, though even in the first team there have been moments when the red mist has descended.

From being one of the heroes when we played Everton at the back end of the 1998-99 season, I found myself cast in the role of villain when the rivalry was renewed at the start of the new campaign. The first red card of my professional career came in the final minutes of a 1-0 defeat at Anfield. Tensions were already running high with Liverpool goalkeeper Sander Westerveld and Everton's Franny Jeffers having both been sent off for an earlier flare-up when I caught Kevin Campbell with a high challenge. In my defence, my foot was high to protect myself because Campbell was coming at me at force. But when he was left in a heap, I knew I was in trouble.

Making a challenge like that is a bit like scoring a goal or making a good tackle. It is a split-second decision, but in this instance I got it wrong. From where the flashpoint took place to the tunnel at Anfield was probably no more than 25 yards, yet it seemed like an eternity as I trudged off. I didn't need people telling me I had been wrong and, by the same token, I didn't need anyone trying to lift my spirits by saying it didn't matter. I was able to put the sending off into context myself. I would now serve a ban, and being deprived of the opportunity to go onto the pitch killed me and told me what I needed to do.

> **"**
> **On the pitch, I became someone I didn't like.**
> **"**

My first walk of shame was not my last and while the challenge on Campbell didn't look good, it wasn't one of my worst.

The tackles I subsequently made on Aston Villa's George Boateng and Everton's Gary Naysmith make me cringe when I see them now.

It is all about finding the right balance. When I was growing up I was always told to let the opposition know you are around early on. Win the battle and you'll win the match. A lot of games in my early years were won through intimidating players. Nowadays you can't do that because you don't stay on the pitch. I have experienced that enough times. Football has changed and you become less aggressive because of the rule changes regarding tackling from behind and approaching challenges with your feet off the floor. But I would say that a competitive instinct is missing in a lot of the kids coming through these days and that, in my opinion, is one of the main reasons why the production line at Liverpool's Academy has slowed in recent times.

To stand out from the rest of the people in your age group, you have to have something extra, something that they have not got. You have to be prepared to run the extra yard when you're physically shattered, make the tackle when it's easier not to and continue to push yourself when really you know you could probably get away with blending into the background.

It is not just about ability. It is about something inside. I look at Michael Owen and he had that instinct when he was growing up. Jamie Carragher had it and I think I had it as well. My problem was that, whatever it was, I had too much of it to begin with.

Can't Believe I've Just Done That

My face says it all. Kevin Campbell is left flat out after I caught him towards the end of a typically fierce Merseyside derby at Anfield. It was a bad tackle and I deserved to be shown the red card by referee Mike Riley. I was guilty of getting carried away and trying to impress too much. To make things worse, we lost that game 1-0. I left Anfield all sheepish, but to compound matters I was having a meal afterwards and who did I bump into in the toilets of the restaurant? Kevin Campbell. I went up to him and apologised in person because obviously I didn't really see him immediately after the game. He could have made it difficult for me, but to be fair to him he was brilliant and we shook hands.

I KNEW I HAD TO MAKE A STATEMENT

Needless to say my sending off against Everton was not what I had in mind, but there was still enough time to ensure the 1999-2000 season was the one where I cemented myself in the Liverpool team.

During the summer I'd had four or five weeks to regroup and assess where I was. I'd had a wonderful taste of what life as a Liverpool player was like, but I was aware that my first full season would constitute a different challenge.

When you break into the first team people will make allowances. Not your team-mates so much, but the manager and coaching staff certainly, and the fans as well. But I knew I had to improve and show I could cope with the demands of playing for Liverpool every three to four days. Not only that, but starting matches as well. I was fortunate in the sense that, right from the start, Gerard Houllier believed in me. He liked me and I knew that if I did the right things, I could always count on his support. My career was shaped over the next 18 months, largely because of Gerard, and that is why I will always owe him such a debt of gratitude.

I learnt how to behave on and off the pitch. I discovered how important diet and rest were and, generally, I came to respect the opportunity that stretched out before me. Cut corners and I could fall by the wayside, but with dedication and professionalism Gerard told me I could be whatever I wanted to be.

From that moment on, there was never any doubt as to which route I would take. Gerard trusted me, but he still took a huge interest in the life I was living. In truth, he probably spent too much of his time checking on me.

He treated me like a son and it was as if I spent half of the day with my 'surrogate dad' and the rest of the day at home with my real mum and dad. Every single day without fail he would want to catch up with me and because of that daily routine the good habits he wanted me to cherish were drilled into me.

Don't get me wrong, he knew I was young and young lads like their downtime. He didn't want me to live like a monk. But he would stress the importance of eating well, resting well and not partying every week.

This was someone who had worked with the top French players, players who had just won the World Cup and would win the European Championship that season. Gerard thought I had the ability to be recognised as a top player as well. I would have been thick not to listen and take in the advice he offered.

But it wasn't a love-in. I was scared of Gerard in those early days and scared of Phil Thompson, his assistant, as well. They were my bosses at the end of the day. My career was in their hands. Yes, they had a lot of confidence in me, but they weren't afraid to give me a lecture either if they felt I wasn't doing it. It certainly wasn't all pats on the back off them. I was desperate to please them and prove them right and I soon chalked up another milestone.

I had always expected my first goal for Liverpool to come from distance. I've had an eye for a shot throughout my career and back when I dreamed about breaking my duck in a red shirt, I envisaged a strike arrowing into the top corner. I was more of a shooter than a finisher. When the moment finally arrived in a match against Sheffield Wednesday in December 1999, it was like nothing I had imagined.

For a start, my first Liverpool goal came from a pass from Rigobert Song which was a surprise in itself. Usually they went over my head! I was midway in my own half and I remember receiving the ball in an area where my first instinct was to look for a pass. That's the way I have always played and especially at that age when I was still looking to feel my way into the team. If there is an easy pass on, I will do it. I only really dribble if I am in a sticky situation or if there is a man to beat and I can get a shot off. I don't go looking to dribble.

But I ran at the Sheffield Wednesday defenders and kept on going as an opportunity opened up in front of me. To be honest, I still expected a last tackle to be made, depriving me of my moment and halting my slalom run, especially when you are taking on the likes of Des Walker, who had been one of the country's top defenders. It didn't, I kept going, and I tucked the chance away.

When the ball hits the back of the net, a weird sensation comes over you. You get lost in a moment, you don't realise what you are doing and, in a sense, you lose control.

This was the type of stuff I would do as a kid when I was coming through the ranks, back when I found everything a little bit easier. Now I was doing it at Anfield, in front of the Sky Sports cameras, and to make things even better my mates – Danny Murphy and

> **For a start, my first Liverpool goal came from a pass from Rigobert Song which was a surprise in itself.**

Davie Thompson – scored in that game as well. It was a huge boost to my confidence. When things like that happen, you realise you can do it at that level and those are the moments that help you grow as a player.

When I was starting out, during my first five, ten, fifteen games, I still had doubts that I might not be able to have a career at Liverpool and that I might get 'found out'. It was all so new, I didn't know what to expect. I suppose feeling like that is just normal, but there would be difficult moments in games and I didn't know for sure that my ability was going to let me cope at that level.

That is why scoring at Anfield was so important for me. All these little things – my debut, my first start and now my first goal – helped me believe in myself a bit more and fill the Liverpool shirt a bit better.

As a team we started to grow as well. We finished fourth, losing on the final day of the season at Bradford to miss out on the Champions League and qualify for the UEFA Cup instead.

Fourth? There was no way I was going to settle for second best let alone fourth, but it represented progress under Gerard and there was a feeling within the squad at the time that we were getting somewhere. Yet no one in the dressing room could have predicted what was to follow.

It's In!

When the ball hit the back of the net for my first goal for Liverpool, I was just lost in the moment. I'd taken a pass, gone round Emerson Thome, evaded Des Walker and finished nicely before diving full length in celebration in front of the fans in the Anfield Road End. I can remember David Thompson, Danny Murphy and Michael Owen piling on top of me. The way they reacted to that landmark moment showed they were almost as pleased as me. Playing for Liverpool was a dream, now scoring for them was something else. As I trotted back into position, my name was read out over the Tannoy and a huge cheer erupted around Anfield. I will never forget that moment.

Me and the Didi Man

Due to the number of foreign players at Liverpool there were, naturally, some cliques in the dressing room. The French lads stuck together for example and, likewise, the English players were a tight group. Danny Murphy, Michael Owen, David Thompson and Jamie

Carragher welcomed me, as did one other – Didi Hamann. It might say he's German on his passport, but he was a Scouser through and through. He knew all the slang and where some foreigners down the years have struggled to understand Carra and myself, he was right in

there with all the banter. As a player, he is one of the best I have played with. Unselfish and very clever, he had this unerring knack of being in the right place at the right time. Here he is congratulating me after my first ever goal for Liverpool against Sheffield Wednesday.

Shadowing a Master

Gazza was coming towards the end of his career when I came up against him, and he was obviously not as good as he was in his prime. But just to say I had been on the same pitch as an England hero was unbelievable. He actually caught me with a sly elbow off the ball in the game, which was out of order, but because it was him I let it go! I would have liked his shirt, but I was too shy to ask for it at that stage of my career. There have been times when I came across him after this tussle. When he was at Everton, he was on the pitch after one derby when we were doing a warm-down and he came up and had a chat. He just said I was a good player and that I should keep doing what I was doing. Then he added with a smile: 'And don't do what I do.'

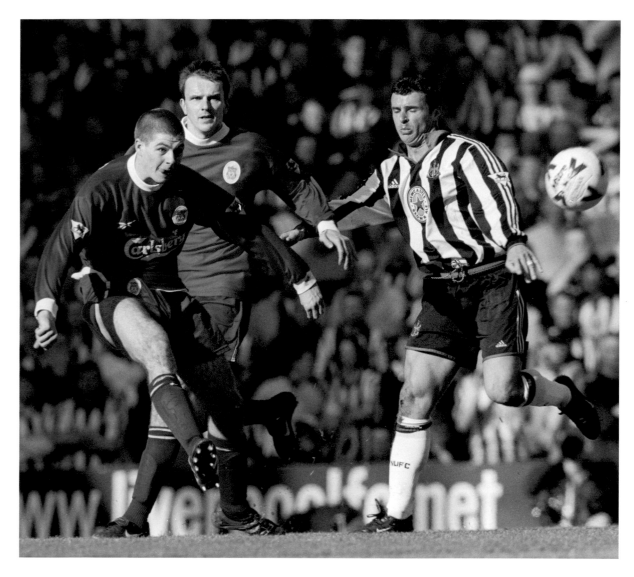

Get In There!

This is probably one of the worst haircuts I have ever seen, but thankfully my shooting was better. I have a good record against Newcastle which overshadows the fact that one of the worst moments of my domestic career came against them. I had just got into the team when we played Newcastle at Anfield in December 1998 (the season before this photo comes from) and I was taken off at half-time just 20 minutes after I had come on as a substitute in the first place. Being brought on and off in the same match is one of the biggest insults to any footballer. I felt terrible. I will always have good memories of Gary Speed and was deeply shocked by his death. I never worried about playing against him when he was in his own half because he kept everything simple, but he had this special ability to run off your blind spot in and around your own penalty area. You would think he was just there, under your control, then the next second he'd head one in the back of the net. A few managers have told me off for that when I played against him. I was guilty of ball watching and then, bang, Gary would punish you with a goal.

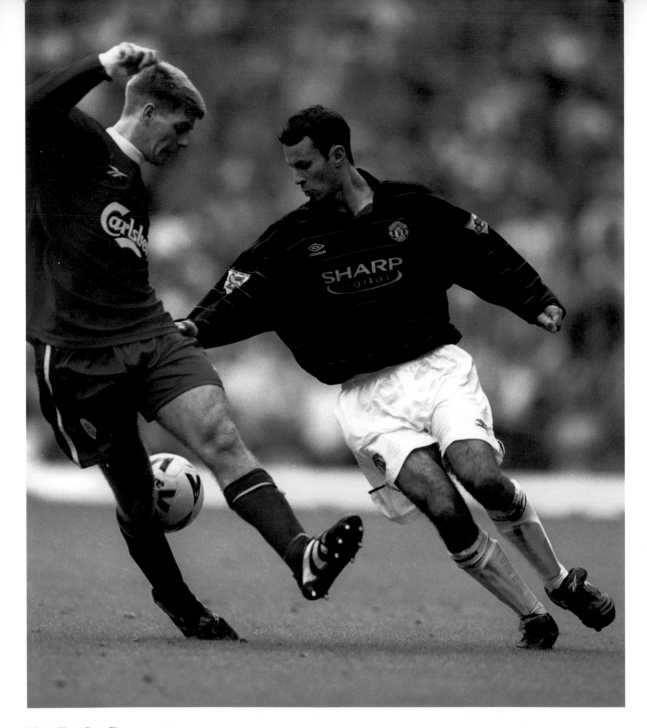

Now You See It ...

There is a strong passion inside me to try and stop Manchester United being successful. They are one of Liverpool's biggest rivals after all. But that doesn't dilute the respect that I have for their players.

I understand the pressure they are under every week to perform and to win trophies. When you have been as successful as they are, you cannot help but acknowledge what they have achieved.

For Ryan Giggs to have played for so long at the very top of his profession is both amazing and a tribute to his hunger and his talent. He is someone I admire immensely.

Up, Up and Away

Heading Is an element of my game I have had to work on. I was small when I was younger and my heading only really started to improve when I had my growth spurt. Whereas tackling and shooting came naturally to me, my aerial strength has definitely developed during my career. I have a natural spring but it's something that I had to bring to my game in order to be an all-round midfielder in the Premier League. When you consider that the most important goal I have scored for Liverpool (against AC Milan in Istanbul) was a header, I must have done something right down the years.

Keeping Up With the Pace

Arsenal has always been a difficult game and in the early days, especially, Patrick Vieira summed them up. In the FA Cup Final in 2001, he wiped the floor with me at times, but overall I felt I held my own in my battles with him. I wouldn't prepare any differently for a game against Arsenal to one against Bolton or Blackburn, for example, but I knew I would have to play to the maximum come Saturday afternoon. Everyone in a Liverpool shirt would have to, otherwise we would lose. One of the most difficult opponents I have ever faced was the Arsenal 'Invincibles' team of 2003-04. They were like a machine. Big, strong and better than most of the teams in the Premier League in every department.

CHAPTER 4

2000
—
2001

THE TREBLE SEASON

There were some mornings before training started, and the banter between the lads hadn't started flying, that if a camera caught me I'd just be gazing around the dressing room at the talent we had: Michael Owen. Jamie Carragher. Robbie Fowler. Jamie Redknapp. Gary McAllister. Danny Murphy. Sami Hyypia. I could go on and on.

I didn't realise we would do quite as well as we did in 2000-2001, a season that became defined by 'The Treble', but I had an inkling that we would compete at the top. It was easy to see the quality that we had in every position, but Gerard Houllier underpinned that by the mentality he was creating.

Professionalism was our watchword. Training was always played at a really high tempo and was very intense. No one wanted to lose a game against their mates, let alone Manchester United or Arsenal on a Saturday afternoon.

People talk a lot in football about having a 'winning mentality'. It is something that is difficult to define, more of a feeling than anything else. Basically, you have so much confidence and trust in the players around you and the manager and coaching staff that you start going into certain games knowing what the result is going to be even before it has kicked off. And, even if the match doesn't start well, or go well at a certain point, you have the confidence and belief that it can be turned round and the momentum tipped back into your favour.

At Liverpool, I've had that feeling a few times. For a spell under Rafa Benitez, I would be training on a Thursday or a Friday and I knew what the score was going to be on the Saturday. I won't name clubs because that is disrespectful, but I knew we would win and I knew what would happen. It was like that under Gerard that season.

Sure, we lost matches, but the feeling of togetherness that we had meant our campaign never unravelled. Gerard had a saying: 'Good teams don't lose twice on the run.' So we didn't and our season got better and better, exceeding our wildest expectations.

Cardiff's Millennium Stadium will always carry happy memories for Liverpool. For a time it seemed like it was our second home.

From the first time we went there in February 2001 to face Birmingham City in the League Cup Final, we had more good times than bad.

It was tight that day and after Robbie Fowler scored early in the match, we slackened off too much. We had been massive favourites going into the match and maybe we thought the result was going to be a foregone conclusion. Darren Purse equalised from the penalty spot in the last minute of normal time and then a shoot-out ensued in which our goalkeeper, Sander Westerveld, emerged as one of Liverpool's heroes.

I must admit there was a certain amount of relief when we lifted the Cup because losing to a side that was a league below us would have been embarrassing and the stick we would have received unrelenting. But, after the game, when we were all back in the hotel celebrating, it dawned on each and every one of us that this was what it is all about.

And especially me. Some of the others had experienced this before, but this was my first final and my first major medal. Of course, I had won medals and trophies growing up and coming through the ranks, and each one is important in its own right, but this felt different. This was like my first proper medal. A place in history.

There is a pressure and a weight of expectation that comes with playing for Liverpool. You are constantly reminded about the history and tradition of the club, what other players have previously won, and I loved the feeling that I was adding to that. Thankfully, there was more, much more, to come. We were back at Cardiff soon after.

I have strong memories of the FA Cup Final while I was growing up: staying in all day as a kid to watch the build-up, and then the match itself, before racing out of the house to the scrap of wasteland on Ironside Road and trying to recreate what I had just witnessed on the TV. Now to be playing in one was a dream come true, although for 83 minutes it was an occasion to endure rather than enjoy.

It was the one-off hardest game I had played in my life at that point. We were physically out of our depth. Arsenal were fitter, stronger and better. Maybe we were tired due to the punishing schedule we had been on, but maybe that's an excuse. Yes it was a tough season, both physically and mentally, but if that final had been played after we'd had four weeks' rest Arsenal would have still played us off the pitch. That pitch was Arsenal's pitch. They were all in their prime and that remains the best Arsenal side ever for me.

I was up against Patrick Vieira that afternoon and it was certainly a learning experience. In the future, I seemed to grow every time I played against him and get better, but back when I was younger he just knew where to be, what to do and if he had wanted to, it felt like he could have gone up a few gears as well.

That we won after being second best for so long was remarkable, although when you have players like Michael Owen on your side the impossible becomes possible. It wasn't a shock to me what he did that afternoon because I had seen Michael do it so many times before at so many different levels. Two chances, two goals. Game over. Freddie Ljungberg had wrapped one hand around the Cup for Arsenal with a goal in the 72nd minute, but Michael came good twice in five minutes after that to underline just how big a player he was.

I had worked with him full-time since leaving school and I knew how mentally strong he was, how fierce he was, how much he detested losing, how much of a battler he was. Arsenal knew that too and still couldn't stop him.

Ordinarily, we would have partied long into the night, but there was the small matter of the UEFA Cup Final against Spanish side Alaves now looming. Two down, one to go.

Liverpool went through the card that season, playing every single game – all 63 of them – as mapped out when the fixtures had been published the previous June. It was a slog, but what an experience.

The UEFA Cup Final was played at Borussia Dortmund's Westfalenstadion and what sticks out in my mind the most was how much Gerard Houllier wanted it. He was delighted to win the Carling Cup and the FA Cup and knew they were important milestones for the club, but he was desperate to lift the UEFA Cup.

> **" That season we put our names in the history books. "**

He was forever talking about European competitions and how hard it is to win a European trophy. I knew we wouldn't let him down.

It took ages to get into the ground because our supporters had taken over. They were literally rocking the bus as we weaved our way through the crowds, wishing us good luck, and you could see in the faces of Michael Owen, Didi Hamann, Markus Babel and players like that just how much they were up for it. Liverpool's supporters had been unbelievable in Cardiff, but this was something else.

We set off like a steam train and after Markus had given us an early lead, I crashed home a second goal following a great pass from Michael of all people. It was meant to be the other way round – me feeding him – but I didn't mind that little bit of role reversal. When I get the licence to burst forward, I can be a goal threat in any game. I played on the right in Dortmund, but with a fair amount of freedom to go where I wanted because we had Didi and Gary McAllister holding in midfield.

However, there was a pattern emerging to our appearances in finals that still holds true today. At Liverpool, we seem to enjoy making life difficult for ourselves.

The scoring was crazy that night. Twice we threw away two-goal leads and then conceded an equaliser in the last minute to take the game into extra time. But even though it must have been torture for Gerard and our fans, I knew we were going to win.

Sure enough, Gary McAllister's free-kick was inadvertently headed into his own net by Alaves' Delfi Geli for what was the 'golden goal'. We exploded in celebration. An insane game to cap an insane season, but one I look back on with immense pride.

Liverpool Football Club is about winning trophies and that season we put our names in the history books alongside the likes of Liddell, St John, Yeats, Dalglish, Rush and Souness.

Right Place, Right Time

A header against our neighbours from across the Mersey, Tranmere Rovers, helped to keep us on course for the cup Treble in 2000-01. The build-up to the game had been huge. John Aldridge, the former Liverpool striker, was the Tranmere manager and a few of their players had come out with the old 'welcome to hell' slogans warning that they would kick us off the pitch.

We played well that day though, winning 4-2, and if you study the starting line-up, you'll notice that Gerard Houllier picked eight British players in his first eleven. He knew it would be a physical battle to begin with and what his selection tells you is that even managers who sign a lot of foreign players know that in certain games they will find it hard to cope without enough home-grown muscularity.

Diving Right In

Another diving celebration came after one of the best strikes I have ever hit. To score against Manchester United at Anfield is always special. To score past a World Cup winning goalkeeper such as Fabian Barthez is pretty special too. But when you put those two things together and add in the fact that the shot from 30 yards was still rising as it hit the top corner of the net, it makes it one of my best goals for Liverpool. To claim a win and three points meant it was a good day all round.

First Goal in Europe

Gerard Houllier gave me licence to get forward into the penalty area from midfield and I knew Didi Hamann would hold the fort behind me if I fancied getting into the box. It is only when you start making those sort of runs that you add goals to your game. I should have scored a few more headers in my career, but my first European goal came from one in a 2-2 draw with Olympiakos in Athens in November 2000 in the UEFA Cup.

Finding My Feet

The hurdles en route to our UEFA Cup success in 2001 grew steadily higher, but I loved every minute of it. Here, I am in action against Porto during a 0-0 stalemate in the first leg of the quarter-final. I found European games, especially those away from home, demanding but stimulating. The atmosphere was different, the pitch was new to me and I didn't know too much about my opponents. In those situations, you have to step up to the mark and, over the years, we have done that at Liverpool in Europe.

McAllister the Master

I admired Gary McAllister from the moment he walked through the door at Anfield and he remains a source of inspiration to me today. Gary is one of the reasons I believe I can carry on at Liverpool if I manage myself correctly and if the club looks after me. Gary wasn't over-trained during his time at the club. He was fresh when he played and that enhanced his tremendous ability to influence games, and not just any games: huge games that shaped Liverpool's history. That is what I want to do. I'm not saying I want to play until I'm 38 or 39, but I'm 32 and between now and when I'm 36, for example, I want to be able to have a big impact at Liverpool.

Taking Aim

My first inclination when I get the ball is to pass it. If one of my team-mates is in a better position than me on the pitch, then I will look to find them rather than selfishly trying to dribble the ball. Technique is important when you are trying to pass accurately, and you can see from how my left ankle is bent over what sort of strain footballers put their bodies under. When you do that repeatedly, it is no wonder you get little niggles and pain in your ankle joints.

Sweet Victory Over United

Winning at Old Trafford is always a cause for celebration and here I am with our goalkeeper, Sander Westerveld. Sander is one of the best goalkeepers I have seen with the ball at his feet. He was exceptional in that respect. But I felt he sometimes looked for an excuse if he ever made a mistake in a game. For me, it is better to say, 'Sorry lads, that was down to me.' He'd try to blame it on something else. When we lost at Middlesbrough once on a freezing day in December, he said there was ice on the ball and that had prevented him from gathering the ball properly. Despite that, he did well for us in the Treble season in 2000-01. He was a good keeper.

The Ignominy of an Early Bath

The walk of shame is a long one and every yard feels like a mile. I've done it quite a few times, too many to be honest. On this occasion, I was sent off against Leeds United at Anfield in April 2001. I was given my marching orders for two bookings, although I will always contend that I didn't deserve either of them. David Batty, the former England midfielder, stitched me up, I felt. Liverpool versus Leeds was always a big match and the atmosphere was bouncing. In my view, Batty milked the contact from a challenge I made when there wasn't too much there, and I paid the price. If it was a deliberate stitch-up, you can look at it two ways. Either he's clever because he laid the bait and I fell for the trap he set, or you can say he was out of order. If I am injured I will stay down but, if he wasn't hurt, I would never have done to him what I felt he did to me.

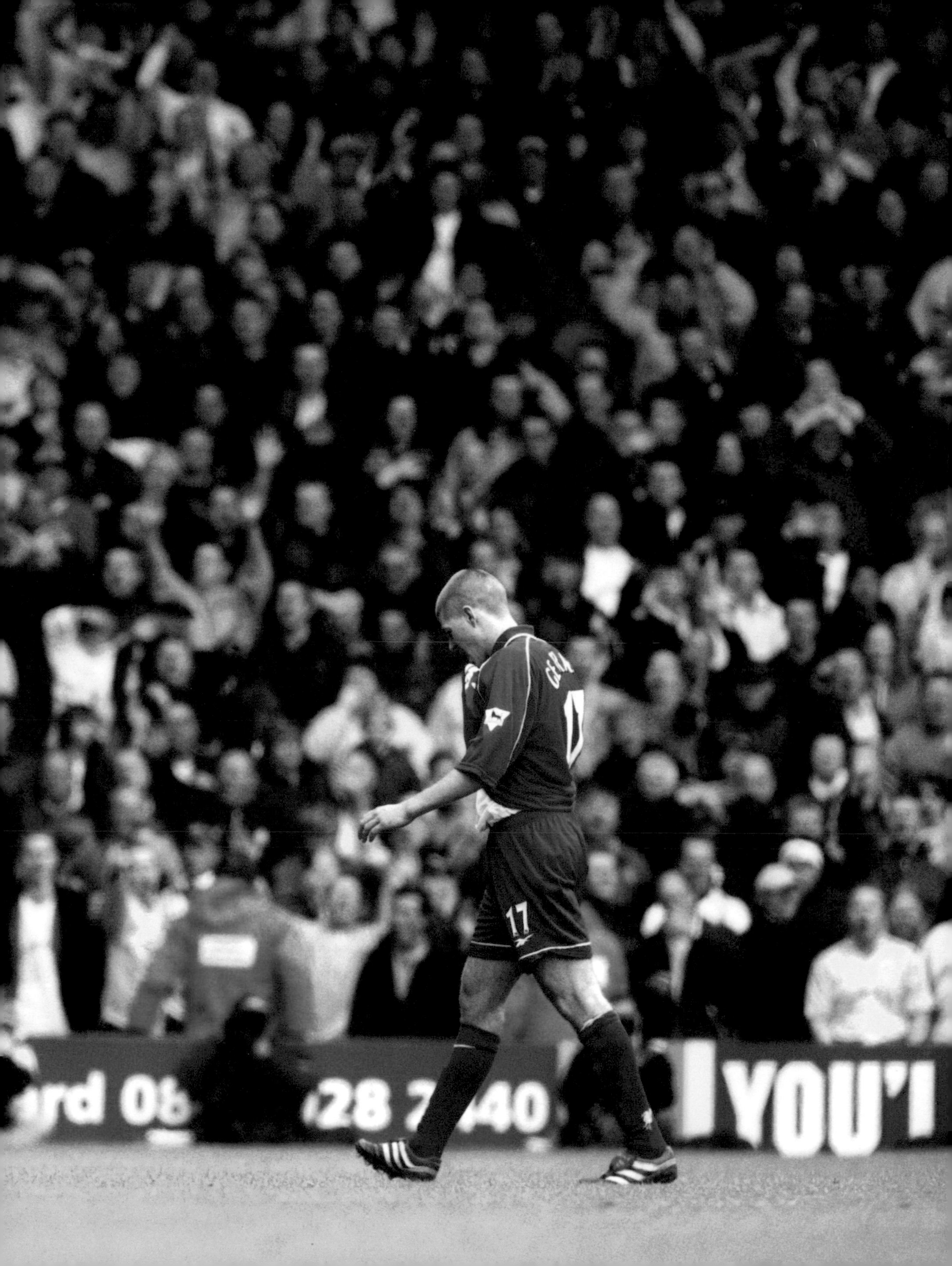
17
YOU'I

Premature End

My first final for Liverpool came against Birmingham City in the League Cup in February 2001, and it set the tone for so many of those that have followed. We made desperately hard work of getting over the line and lifting the trophy.

Robbie Fowler gave us an early lead with an amazing volley, but we couldn't shake Birmingham off and ended up needing penalties to prevail. I was on the bench by then, having been taken off after 78 minutes.

Unplayable Robbie

Robbie was captain that day and his volleyed goal from 30 yards was brilliant. He maybe wasn't at his best when I played alongside him, but he was still very good. In training no one else could have duplicated some of the goals he scored because of the power he got into his shots with virtually no back-lift. His accuracy to hit the inside of the net from tight angles remains the best I have seen to this day. There were times when a game of 5-a-side would begin in training and after 10 seconds you'd be 2-0 down because Robbie had banged in two goals. Turn finish, turn finish. You'd be left thinking to yourself, 'We might as well stop this now because he's unplayable.'

Calming the Pre-match Nerves

It is important to learn from your mistakes and I'm glad to say there was no repeat of the infamous white FA Cup Final suits of 1996 when we played in the final in 2001. Everything was a lot more toned down. Stephen Wright (far right) came through the ranks with me and Robbie, and Jamie Redknapp helped to look after us both during the build-up.

In the days before a major final, you mentally prepare yourself for the game and the fact that we were playing Arsenal meant we knew we would have to be on our mettle. But before the game you can still be pretty calm and relaxed. It is only when you are in the dressing room that the butterflies and the nerves start and you realise exactly what is at stake.

Late and Lethal – Michael's Day

The faces say it all. There is joy written across all of our features, but surprise as well at having turned round a game we were second best in. Arsenal had taken the lead through Freddie Ljungberg and with seven minutes left we were still trailing at Cardiff's Millennium Stadium, having not done ourselves justice. But that was Michael Owen for you. He could come alive in an instant and bang, bang he turned the game on its head. We owed him an awful lot that day.

A Childhood Dream

As a kid I used to stay glued to the TV when it was FA Cup Final day. Afterwards, whoever had won, I would pretend to be one of their players in the street outside my house. It sounds a cliché but it was a dream of mine to win the FA Cup and, of course, you never think you are ever going to achieve it. It is an experience that's difficult to describe properly, but it's magical, that's for sure. I have this picture in a room at my house together with Patrick Vieira's shirt from the game. They're in the same frame. A nice memento.

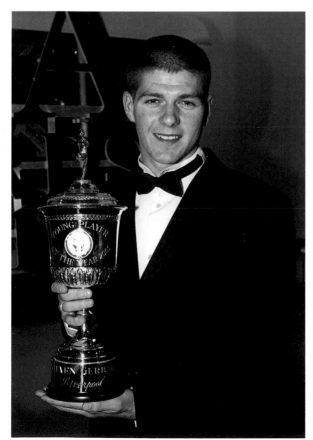

Early Recognition

I played 50 games and scored 10 goals in the 2000-01 season and things could hardly have gone better for me. As well as the Treble, I won the PFA Young Player of the Year award. Team honours are always more important to me and I realised that without the support of my team-mates there was no way I would have been recognised. There are pitfalls to being lauded and showered with accolades, but I knew I had to stay on the straight and narrow and make the most of the talent I had. I wanted to win more trophies with Liverpool first and foremost, and if that led to individual honours, all well and good. Later on, in 2006, I won the PFA Players' Player of the Year and to receive both awards in your career is an achievement I am proud of. Not many players have done that.

Final Flourish

I am proud of my record of scoring in big matches. I've found the net in the League Cup Final, FA Cup Final and European Cup Final with Liverpool, and in the World Cup finals with England. The run started here in the UEFA Cup Final in Dortmund in 2001 when we beat Spanish side Alaves. My goal was something of a rarity because Michael played me in with a great ball. I have to say, it was about time he returned the favour! Over time my finishing has improved but when I got into positions such as this early in my career I just wanted to hit the ball as hard as I could. If a centre forward had had the same chance, maybe he would have placed it. But as a midfielder, who wasn't used to having only the goalkeeper to beat, you tend to blast it – that is why I was so far off the floor. The game itself was another rollercoaster. We should have had it tied up in normal time, but let them back in and ended up winning 5-4 by virtue of a 'golden goal' in extra time. Winning all three cup competitions we entered that season often gets overlooked, but it was a fantastic achievement.

CHAPTER 5

2001
2002

GERARD
MY HERO

The night we lifted the UEFA Cup to complete our
Treble season, I was ready to party. Gerard Houllier had
other ideas.

We still had one game left – away at Charlton
Athletic – and one that would determine whether
we would be defending our European trophy next
season or rubbing shoulders with the big boys in the
Champions League. This wasn't the time for beers and
champagne. Gerard put us on lockdown. He told us
to be patient and then we could party.

At the time, the lads and myself didn't understand.
We'd just written a glorious chapter in Liverpool's history
and wanted to be let off the leash. I thought the
manager was being a killjoy and I didn't appreciate
fully how important the Champions League was at that
point. But without him, we would not have qualified to
join Europe's élite. There is no question about that. If we
as players had had our way, I doubt we would have
won 4-0 at Charlton just a few days after the Alaves
game and finished third in the table. As always Gerard's
professionalism shone through and he guided us over
the line.

When you consider how important Gerard was to
Liverpool, then for him to suffer a life-threatening illness
just three months into the new season was upsetting
and worrying for everyone. We came in at half-time of
a game against Leeds United at Anfield in October 2001
expecting him to be there as always and impart some
more words of wisdom. Even when we were told he had
been taken ill, I, for one, thought he'll just get it checked
and then he'll be fine. It wasn't until we spoke to the
club doctor, Mark Waller, that we grasped just how
serious the heart problem he had was.

I was worried about what would happen to Gerard
and then I worried about what would happen to us as
a team. We had all been on an upward curve, winning
trophies and making giant strides, and I did wonder
if his illness would derail us and lead to us caving in.
But his battle for health was the most important thing.
I don't know how all the players felt, but I missed
him enormously. He had been there for me every
day since I broke into the first team set-up and I
missed his reassuring presence, asking how I was,
giving me little tips, telling me what I was doing both
right and wrong.

It was typical of Gerard that he was sending text
messages to the team as soon as possible and sooner
than the doctors would have allowed had they known.
'Keep playing well. I'm OK, I'll be back soon', were the
sort of messages he sent. Again, it was typical of Gerard
that he thought of others before assuring you that he
would be OK. He was more interested in the team than
himself, which is amazing really when you consider how
his life was in danger. That is impressive.

My concerns about whether our season would
unravel without Gerard were unfounded and did not
factor in Phil Thompson's capabilities as coach.

We had a lot of foreign players in the squad –
Sami Hyypia, Markus Babbel, Vladimir Smicer – and I
suppose I wondered whether Thomo would be able to
maintain the atmosphere and harmony that had built
up between us all.

We had just won the Treble, but already that season
we had added the Charity Shield, beating Manchester
United, and the European Super Cup, beating Bayern
Munich, to our expanding silverware collection. It was
a big challenge for Thomo to come in and take the
reins alone, but he was brilliant and did an
unbelievable job.

You couldn't challenge him because he had lifted
the European Cup as captain in Paris in 1981 and won
so many other trophies and titles that it was ingrained in

him exactly what the club stood for. Anyone looking to pinch an inch and cut some corners in Gerard's absence didn't stand a chance and so we continued making strides.

There were set-backs, however. Barcelona came to Anfield in the second group phase of the Champions League and played us off the park, winning 3-1 despite Michael opening the scoring. It was mind blowing how they moved the ball and how different their style was to our own. Xavi played, but it was Patrick Kluivert and Marc Overmars who did the damage.

After matches like that you start doubting yourself and the team. I thought to myself leaving Anfield that night, 'What level can I get to because these players seem to be on a different one from me?'

But you dig in and recover and as the season progressed we were still in the hunt to win the league and the Champions League.

Gerard had returned to the dug-out on an emotional night against AS Roma when we needed to win by two clear goals to remain in Europe. He would admit now that he came back too soon, but that he did so showed the strength of the bond he had with the club. He wanted to be in the dug-out, helping, guiding his team. Still, his presence helped us that night with Jari Litmanen scoring a penalty and then Emile Heskey sealing our progress and leading Gerard to proclaim later we were 'ten games from greatness'. We came up short.

Bayer Leverkusen beat us 4-3 on aggregate in the Champions League quarter-finals before we came

> **"It was typical of Gerard that he thought of others before assuring you that he would be OK."**

second behind Arsenal in the Premier League, finishing seven points behind Arsene Wenger's side. After all the highs we had grown used to, the disappointment was numbing.

For me, the pain manifested itself in other ways as well. All throughout my career, problems with my fitness have repeatedly cropped up.

The first serious set-back I endured came on the final day of the 2001-02 season. I had been nursing a groin injury for some time, but given the importance of the games Liverpool were competing in I played through the pain barrier.

There was also the World Cup coming up with England in Japan and South Korea and there were people saying to me to wait until after the tournament and then have surgery.

The pressure they were putting on me left me with a decision to make. Do I get the injury sorted and come back the player I want to be at the start of the next season for Liverpool? Or do I go to the World Cup carrying an injury, not being able to train and go into the games maybe 50% fit, then get judged on those performances and miss a big chunk of the next season?

When I put it like that it seems straightforward. In the event, the decision was taken out of my hands.

I broke down on the final weekend of the campaign in a home game with Ipswich and I knew as I trudged off that England was no longer an option. It was a tough moment for me, but throughout the summer one thought kept me going: I was confident that we could challenge for the league.

A Special Rivalry

What you don't see in this picture is that I have my tongue out as I run along the front of the Bullens Road stand at Goodison Park down to the corner where the Liverpool fans are. I had been abused by Evertonians throughout the game. They had thrown coffee at me, and half-eaten sausage rolls, and I actually got hit by a coin on the bridge of my nose. It hurt, but the only thing you can do is try to make their team suffer. I rifled one into the top corner and the celebration wasn't just instinct. It was to say: 'Throw whatever you want at me … there you go, there's my reaction.'

The Art of Crossing

The way I look to cross a ball, I take risks because I want to put a certain amount of pace on it. I can hit the right area 10 times out of 10 if my cross is slow or floated, but I try to put in balls with pace and venom so that they are enticing for my team-mates. Sometimes you can't get them right, but I have the confidence now that if one goes off-target the next one will be better. My delivery from wide areas is an important part of my game. You can catch opponents out if you hit the ball early and with power into the right area.

Bulking Up

I'm trying my luck from distance here against Everton, but if you look at the difference in my physique now to when I made my debut the contrast is stark. The change is down to Gerard Houllier. I hate the gym. I find it boring. Unfortunately, due to the injuries that I have had in recent seasons, I have done more gym work in the last 12 months than I ever did between the ages of 22 and 28.

I never used to go in partly because of the back problems I have had earlier in my career. But when I started out, Houllier said that if I wanted to play for him in the middle of midfield then I needed to bulk up a bit. You can see the definition in my quad muscles which you get from doing squats holding weights. I am starting to get the build of a strong Premier League player.

Jamie – a Great Player and Mentor

Jamie Redknapp had the body I wanted. I was a similar height to him and when I broke into the first team, I saw how he had the build of a top, top player and I wanted the same. I strived for a physique like his. He suffered a lot from injuries at Liverpool, but he scored a great goal here against Charlton at The Valley and I have tons of respect for him as a player and a person. He has always stayed in touch and I can count on Jamie to be honest with me. When we talk about football, it is not just a case of him giving me a pat on the back. We talk about what I, and the team, have done right and wrong.

Getting a Taste for the Champions League

The UEFA Cup was good to me as a player. I got to lift the trophy and I found out about what playing in Europe was all about. But as soon as you taste the Champions League, you never want to go back. I found the quality of the opposition and the speed of the games went up a notch from what I was used to. There was no hiding place. Sink or swim. You can have a couple of seasons at Liverpool under your belt and think you are doing well, but there is no time to sit back and take it in. There were always new challenges to confront and conquer.

This is during a game against Borussia Dortmund in our first season in the competition in 2001-02, and I loved everything about the Champions League. I didn't dare to dream at that point it would provide me with the best moment of my career.

Rising to the Physical Challenge

When I was starting out, I probably would have ended up in a heap next to the advertising hoardings at the side of the pitch following this tussle. I wasn't timid, but I wasn't strong enough for the cut and thrust of the Premier League. The physical demands on players these days are immense. Every game is a battle. I needed to get stronger in order to win these sorts of situations and then showcase the talent that I have. I'm shoulder to shoulder here with a Blackburn defender and, hopefully, I'm just about to get the better of him.

Finesse, Not Power

Where Jussi Jaaskelainen is concerned I have a lucky streak. I have scored more goals against him – seven – than against any other goalkeeper in my career. This one against Bolton was different from the sort of powered finish I normally produce. My finishing has improved with experience. When you find yourself in certain positions in front of goal, you are a little bit more calm and relaxed as opposed to when you first get into the team. Practising helps, but I have to be careful how long I stay behind after training because of the injuries I have had. It is about quality not quantity.

Celebrating with a Good Friend

I'm very rarely in touch with Michael Owen these days. I suppose that's natural in a sense because he left Liverpool in 2004 to move to Real Madrid. I can totally understand why he made that switch. Real are one of the biggest clubs in the world, if not the biggest, and Michael was a success there even though he only spent one season at the Bernabeu. I have to be honest and say I was very surprised he chose to sign for Manchester United. Michael enjoyed legendary status at Liverpool, but that has been diluted now because of the move he made. Only Michael knows if he got that decision right.

Battling for Possession

This was when Chelsea started to
become a really powerful force.
They signed a lot of foreign players
who had real quality and you knew
when you faced them it was going
to be a tough game and a physical
battle like the one I'm having here
with William Gallas. Chelsea, Arsenal
and Manchester United were bigger
and stronger than the other teams
in the Premier League around this
time which gives an insight into the
quality and type of players they buy
and also how much is at stake.
I don't think you'd get the neutrals
saying Liverpool-Chelsea was a
great game too often. They have
always been attritional matches, with
the teams cancelling each other out.

World Cup Dreams Torn Apart

Walking off, head down, with the Liverpool physio Dave Galley, I knew I would not be going to the World Cup with England in 2002. A concerned Gerard Houllier is behind me. We played Ipswich on the final day of the season and the injuries that had been affecting me towards the end of that campaign became too much.

I damaged my groin and the decision was taken the next day that I would undergo surgery, which meant a lay-off during the summer. I was gutted to miss out on going to such a big tournament, but if I had tried to cover up the problem I knew I wouldn't have done myself – or the country – justice.

A Footballing Lesson

This picture is a rarity because it captures one of the five or six touches I managed to get against Barcelona in the Nou Camp! Even now I remember something really clearly from one of my first games there. One of us hoofed the ball into space up the pitch and Sammy Lee, who was part of Gerard Houllier's backroom staff, shouted: 'Good decision.' Normally the thought of surrendering possession would be frowned upon by Liverpool coaches, but the reason it was a good decision was that it allowed us to breathe and get to the halfway line. That shout sticks in my head. Barcelona have a way of playing that is deep in their culture. When they are kids, they are embarrassed when they give the ball away and so you see them cherish possession. When you play against Barcelona it is usually a long night.

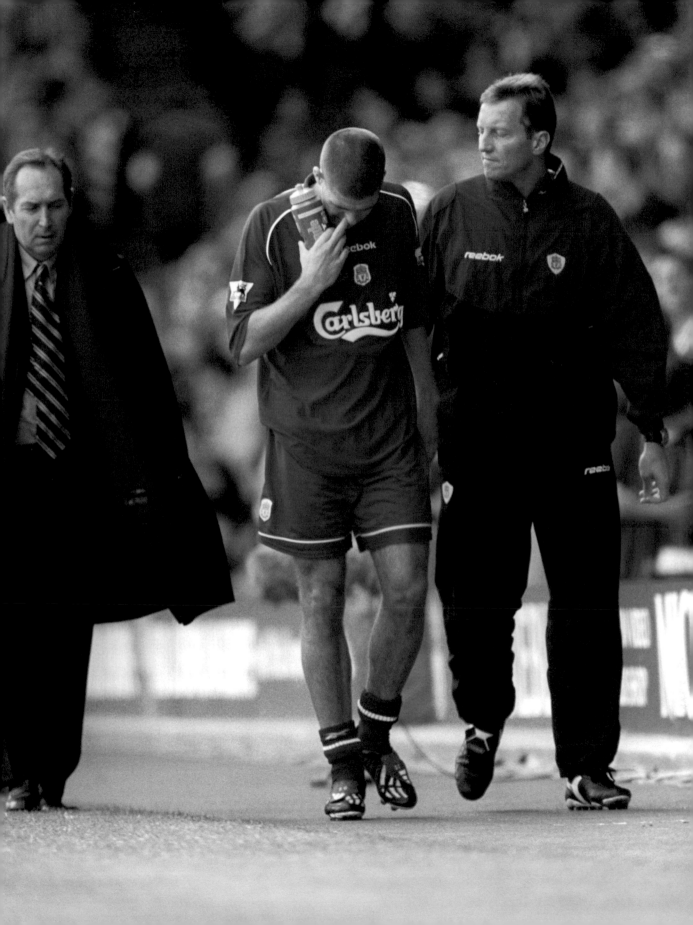

CHAPTER 6

2002
—
2003

MISSED OPPORTUNITIES

You train all week, rest well, eat well, prepare well, and you know exactly what you want to do. But there remain some things which, as a footballer, are still out of your control.

Liverpool had really good players, and some great ones, at the time we were winning the Treble and making progress in the league. We had grown together over a period of three or four years and I think that if the club had added to that with a couple of key signings we could have won the title.

It is a regret that this wasn't the case, but, as I say, sometimes as players you can only do so much. Of all the seasons back when Michael was terrorising defences, I think 2002-03 was the one where we missed out. We had finished second to Arsenal and were ready to push on. Unfortunately, the signings we made that summer did not come off.

You work out pretty quickly whether a new team-mate is going to cut it or not simply by training alongside them. My first impressions of El-Hadji Diouf, Salif Diao and Bruno Cheyrou, signed for combined fees of £18m, were not good. I only wish I had been wrong and it had turned out that I judged them too soon.

I knew Diao was tough. I knew he would do a job in certain games and be a decent squad player, but I thought he wasn't good enough to play every week. You could trust him and you knew what you were going to get from him. He put in a few good performances for Liverpool, but the way I look at it, to play for Liverpool in the centre of midfield you have to be very good and perform consistently. That's my opinion. He had caught the eye with Senegal in the World Cup in Japan that summer, but he wasn't world class.

I felt sorry in some respects for Cheyrou. The moment Gerard claimed he was the next Zinedine Zidane, he was on a hiding to nothing. Yes he was French – we'd signed him from Lille – but the comparison with one of the best players ever to have played killed him from the start. How could it not? Cheyrou is a nice guy and he had talent, but he wasn't suited to the Premier League in the same way that Alberto Aquilani later found it tough.

Diouf was the biggest surprise for me because I remember we had the chance to sign Nicolas Anelka permanently. He had joined on loan in the second half of the previous season and made an impact, quickly becoming a favourite with the players and the fans. Gerard called a group of us into a room one day and said he had the chance to sign Anelka before adding that he was getting Diouf instead, that we'd all love him and that he'd turn out to be a class addition for us. That is one of the few things I can ever criticise Gerard for. He got that decision wrong.

As for 'loving' Diouf? I found him a constant liability to me and the rest of my team-mates. He wasn't the type of person, or player, I wanted in the dressing room with us and the way his career has since gone isn't a surprise to me. I thought he was arrogant and massively over-rated. I desperately wanted to win the Premier League, we all wanted to win the Premier League, and basically he was compromising that ambition. There were rare occasions when he played well, more often than not when he was moved on to the right of midfield. Yet he had been bought from Lens to score the goals that would take us from second place to the summit. He had been recruited to make the difference. That didn't happen.

Selfishly, you do feel let down by the club. Just as the supporters do. We were close to taking a step forward and ended up taking two or three backwards.

I had started the season with such high hopes, but the whole campaign turned into a rollercoaster with more lows than highs.

Even though Liverpool did not lose a Premier League game until the start of November, I knew things weren't right. We weren't going to move on to the next level after all.

There were some silver linings. We won the League Cup, beating Manchester United 2-0 at Cardiff, after I had given us the lead with a deflected shot from distance that flew past Fabian Barthez. Michael sealed victory with time running out. Any time you beat United is great and that it came in a final meant it was even better. I had another winners' medal. But, in the context of our season, winning the League Cup was the bare minimum we had set our sights on.

Personally, I found that season tough. I suffered a dip in form that resulted in me being hauled off in a Champions League match against FC Basle which Liverpool had to win to stay in the competition. At half-time we were 3-0 down. I'd stunk in the first half and Gerard told me to get showered at the break. It was an embarrassing performance from me. Liverpool needed to drag themselves off the canvas and I wasn't deemed worthy of helping my team-mates out. That was a big blow. A slap in the face. Instinctively, you go on the defensive when that happens. I blamed the manager. I wanted to take on Gerard and Phil Thompson as I sat sulking in the dressing room, believing the whole world was against me.

> **Any time you beat United is great and that it came in a final meant it was even better. I had another winners' medal.**

It was a big deal at the time, a story that gripped the media because afterwards Gerard publicly questioned whether I had got too big for my boots. That hurt.

It was days, maybe weeks, later that I realised I was taken off for the right reasons and the Liverpool staff were trying to help me.

I realised that I wasn't playing well and it wasn't anyone else's fault but my own. It was a problem I had to rectify myself and stop searching for excuses. Liverpool came back to draw 3-3 in Basle, although it wasn't enough for us to remain in the Champions League. Some 10 years on and I still think about that night from time to time. It is moments like those that spur me and drive me on so that it doesn't happen again. You go back to the drawing board.

Sometimes you think you have learnt all you can learn and then: smack. Something happens and you realise, 'Hang on, I'm still wet behind the ears.'

It wasn't just the Basle game that did that to me. That season was the first time I came across Rafa Benitez. He was the coach of Valencia, who had just won La Liga in Spain, breaking up the heavyweight dominance of Real Madrid and Barcelona.

We were drawn in the same Champions League group as them and lost home and away, barely getting a kick. They dominated from start to finish, pressed the ball and basically suffocated us. They were the methods I would experience at first hand later on, but for the time being Rafa had left me worried. Seeing the standard they set made me realise Liverpool needed to be better. An awful lot better. We were falling short against the best. That meant we had to improve.

Taking on a Daunting Adversary

Arsene Wenger complained about this tackle on Patrick Vieira in a Charity Shield match in the curtain raiser to the 2002-03 season. He has his opinion, but I never hear him saying much when one of his own players has made a hard tackle. This game was one of the first times the two teams had met since the FA Cup Final when we were played off the park but still nicked the trophy. It was clear I had two options. Either you stand off them again and we don't get lucky this time, or you get in their faces and make it hard for them. I chose the latter.

Rough and Tumble

Hitching a lift on Charlton's Scott Parker, who later became my team-mate with England at Euro 2012. We had a decent partnership in the tournament. Scenes like this are part and parcel of the cut and thrust of the Premier League. I don't know how I got on top of him, presumably I was going for a header at some point, and I'm on the way down.

Overstepping the Mark

Squaring up to Kevin Campbell in a Merseyside derby – again – after a poor tackle on Gary Naysmith, who is lying on the turf out of shot. You'll notice a certain Wayne Rooney trying to get involved. It was Wayne's first Merseyside derby and the Everton fans had been singing all through the game, 'Rooney's gonna get you.' He bounced our goalkeeper, Chris Kirkland, in one full-blooded challenge and also hit the bar. He was desperate to make his mark. I had seen Wayne in junior games, and word was spreading fast that he was a special player. It's amazing to think that not long after this I was playing with him for England.

With a Little Help From My Freund

I am either trying to win a free-kick against Steffen Freund here or looking to run the ball out of play and give my team-mates a breather. To me this is a classic Premier League photograph. Rough and tumble, no one giving an inch. There are a lot of strong players in the top flight and you have to try to hold your own. If you don't, it's simple: you get bullied and then disappear.

Always There With a Helpful Word

Gerard was the manager and I was just a player, but at times our relationship felt as though it was father and son. I like this picture because I think the warmth between us and respect we had for each other comes shining through. Nothing was ever too much trouble for Gerard Houllier where I was concerned and that is still the case today. When England played France at Euro 2012, he was in touch in the build-up, looking to help me because he knew how important that tournament was for me. Yes he's French, but he wasn't being unpatriotic. I think 1-1 was the perfect result for him.

First Taste of Rafa's Talents

Our visit to the Mestella in September 2002 resulted in a performance I would get to know very well. Valencia were coached by Rafa Benitez and the way his team took us apart planted a seed with the Anfield hierarchy. Valencia were hard to beat, they pressed the ball well and had good players in the final third. It was the blueprint Rafa used when he eventually came to Liverpool. We were suffocated in this game, losing 2-0 to goals that were world class.

Adding to the Tally

When you smack a ball as hard
as you can, it naturally brings both
feet off the ground. I have never set
myself a goal-scoring target. When
I first broke into the team, I think if
you got double figures from midfield
that was seen as being really good.
But now the bar has been raised by
players such as Frank Lampard and
Paul Scholes, 15 is almost seen as
the norm.

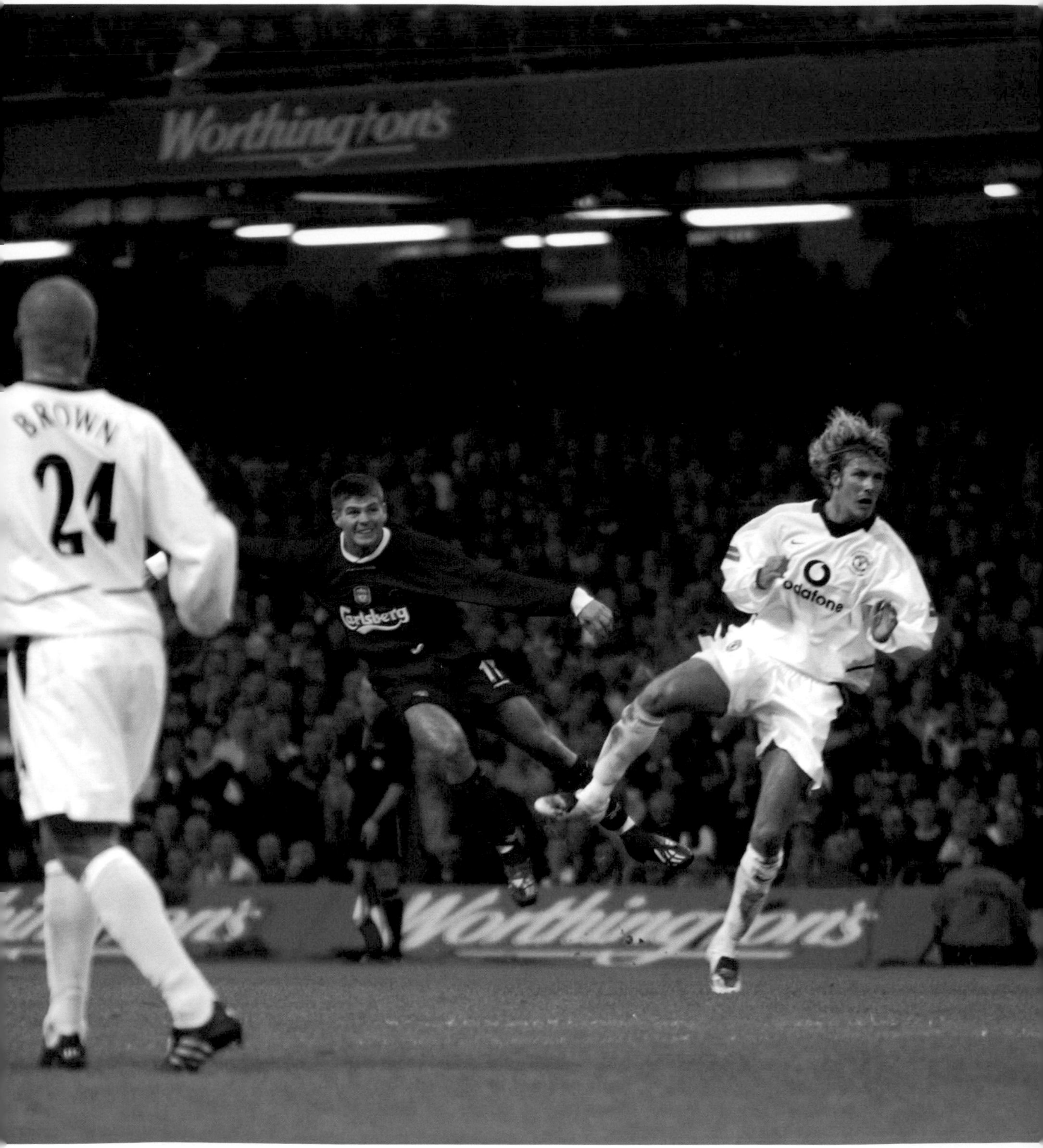
Worthingtons
BROWN
24
Carlsberg
odafone
Worthingtons

The Sweetest Thing

There aren't many better feelings than scoring against Manchester United, especially in a major final. It is important to take the chance to win silverware because it doesn't come round too often and when we played United in the Worthington Cup Final in 2003, I knew we had to seize the moment.

I only ever fear losing to Everton and United because I am a fan and I know how much it hurts, so to win 2-0 was a relief as much as anything. My goal had a bit of luck to it, taking a deflection off David Beckham and looping into the top corner. But I'll settle for that. My celebration was instinctive. Just the perfect day.

It Means So Much

Days like this are everything I dreamed of as a kid: winning silverware, scoring a goal and celebrating with my mates. Michael added another late on to seal the win and we had a good celebration afterwards. At that time under Gerard Houllier, Liverpool had the Indian sign over United. We used to play a diamond formation in midfield, with a holding player for security and then we would end up out-numbering them in the middle. On a big pitch like at Cardiff or at Old Trafford, having more bodies in the middle helped.

CHAPTER 7

2003
2004

FAREWELL HOULLIER

There have been plenty of occasions in my career when I have been asked for my opinion on a manager's situation. What's going on? Can we turn it round? Has he lost the dressing room? I have been asked those questions by fans and I have been asked those questions by people at Liverpool.

But I can honestly say, on my kids' lives, that I have always backed every manager I have worked under. Yes, there have been occasions when I have been frustrated with how things are going and when I have been quizzed about things I could have said: 'This is rubbish. We hate the manager. We want out. The club's going nowhere.' Instead, I have said we can turn it round and I believe I can help whoever is in charge.

I am all for fighting for a manager rather than sticking the knife in and pushing him closer to the sack. So the whispers and the rumours that become fact, especially in a city like Liverpool, that the senior players were behind Gerard Houllier leaving in the summer of 2004 – forget it.

I heard that I was consulted and I had a say in his departure. Not at all. I have gone out of my way on countless occasions to back managers not just through my performances, but in what I say. When results don't go well at a big club like Liverpool everyone sees what is around the corner. As players we have targets, but also the fans and the club have aims and aspirations as well. When you fail to reach them, change becomes inevitable.

There has been a pattern at Liverpool, going back to when I was going to the games as a fan, whereby managers have left.

Ultimately, it is the manager whose job comes under threat because Liverpool's history demands that the team competes at the very top. It is difficult and sad to see anyone in any walk of life lose their job, but when it is someone you have built up a very strong relationship with over the years, someone who has gone out of their way to be supportive of you, it hurts even more.

The harsh reality of football is magnified as well when you are young. Nowadays I am more thick-skinned. I have come to realise that football is a business and that managers come and go in every league in the world. However, when Gerard left there was a huge sense of sadness.

Liverpool finished fourth in the 2003-04 season, which ironically would be considered as a success today, but back then it wasn't viewed as enough. The Premier League has grown stronger and stronger and that season was the first in which the landscape changed.

Roman Abramovich had just bought Chelsea, which was to prove fantastic for them, but a major set-back for everyone else. No one knew that much about Abramovich to begin with, but as the days and weeks went by you started to realise that big changes were taking place within English football.

Money has always talked, but now the sort of sums that were being spent were mind-boggling. Signings were arriving at Stamford Bridge left, right and centre and I realised that while Abramovich was around it was going to take time and be a massive challenge for Liverpool to win the league again.

It didn't seem impossible, but Chelsea immediately established themselves at a level that we were still striving to reach. Overnight they became genuine contenders. I knew they weren't going to go away.

In those circumstances, every pound and penny that Liverpool spent had to be spot on. Yet whereas other teams made signings and improved their squad, becoming stronger, I feel now that we went a bit flat. The margins are fine. If you don't strengthen in the summer correctly, you will find other sides pulling away from you. The sides with the most financial power usually get their signings right because they have first pick of the best players available. Everyone else comes in behind them because they don't want to get involved in a head-to-head battle for players that they cannot realistically win. You get judged on your signings and while it wasn't solely down to Diouf, Diao and Cheyrou that we didn't progress as we wanted, Gerard paid the price.

Yet that final step in football is the hardest. And it is getting even harder to take now. I was gearing up for Euro 2004 with England when the decision was taken by Liverpool's board of directors that Gerard would be leaving.

> **"I can honestly say, on my kids' lives, that I have always backed every manager I have worked under."**

I know the chairman David Moores and Rick Parry the chief executive were sad, even though they were making a decision they felt was in the best interests of the club, and I felt the same way.

From the moment I broke into Liverpool's first team, Gerard spoke to me every day. The conversation I had with him for the first time after it was announced he had left was difficult and awkward. I had shared everything with him and yet now I didn't really know what to say except 'thank you' and 'sorry'.

Typically, Gerard was more interested in me than in himself. 'Keep going, keep learning' was the gist of what he said to me when really I should have been the one offering him kind words. But that is Gerard Houllier for you. Before every big game, a text message will come through from him wishing me good luck. If Liverpool – or England – have a big result, he will be in contact offering his congratulations. He is always in touch to see how my family is and vice versa. I keep in contact with him as well. Just because he left Liverpool did not mean our relationship ended. In many ways, the texts and conversations I have with him now mean more than ever.

Getting Palmed Off

I have taken a few blows to my mouth and face over time, but that comes with wanting to win. Tackling has always been a big part of my game and really I have no right to get to the ball here. I'm helped by the fact that I have got long legs, but being at full stretch probably explains why I have picked up niggles in my groin. Sometimes I'll get the tackle right, other times I'll get it wrong and it'll be a yellow card. This looks like I got it spot on against Tottenham's Helder Postiga, although referee Uriah Rennie probably gave a foul!

Laying My Body on the Line Against the Gunners

Games against Arsenal are always physical and you have to be prepared to win the battle before you can win the match itself. I was trying my utmost to reach a pass here in the Arsenal penalty area, but the ball has evaded me. I've had some good moments against the London club over the years and the odd low point, but I love playing against them and I'll always try my hardest to ensure that it is Liverpool who come away the happier of the two teams.

CAPTAINCY

When Gerard Houllier called me into his office one day, I thought it was just going to be another of those seemingly daily chats about how I was doing. Then he dropped something of a bombshell.

'Stevie, I want you to be captain. I think the time is right for you.' For a split second, I was stunned and shocked. And then excited.

'Great. Fantastic. Of course,' I said. I had worn the armband before. The first time I was captain was in a League Cup tie against Southampton in November 2002 that we won 3-1 at Anfield. But this was different. This was for keeps. It was only after I left Gerard's room that a new emotion washed over me: worry.

This was something I desperately wanted, but questions instantly popped into my head. Would I be any good as a captain? How would the lads react? It wasn't as if my form had been sparkling around that time and there were other senior players who might have deserved that honour.

More importantly, how would Sami Hyypia, who was the current captain, react? From what I could see Sami was doing a good job. Ideally, you don't want to receive the captaincy on account of it being taken off someone else. It is better if a player leaves a club or someone retires after a distinguished career. But Sami still had years ahead of him at Anfield and he had developed into a key player for us since arriving from Dutch club Willem II in 1999.

My respect for him, therefore, only increased as a result of the hand-over of the armband. I knew he was a top guy, but he went up in my estimation afterwards. Not once did he sulk, not once did he make life difficult for me and not once did he let the disappointment he must have felt show. Sami made a decision just to get on with things and he can rightly be described as an Anfield legend.

The hairs on the back of my neck stood up as I walked out for the first time as Liverpool's permanent skipper in a UEFA Cup tie against Olympic Ljubljana on October 15, 2003. It wasn't a bad start either: we won 3-0. My life changed again with the armband on. I went from being a normal player to Liverpool captain at the age of 23.

Looking back, maybe it came too soon and I was too young. Usually captains are aged 25 and over, and coming into their peak years. But one of Gerard's motives for giving it to me at such a young age was that he wanted me to mature that bit quicker because he wanted me to reach my potential. He wanted me to realise the opportunity I had in front of me.

When you are 23 and a Liverpool player, you can still get away with going to certain places and doing certain things. You are under the microscope, but it is not as intense. When you are 23 and you are the Liverpool captain, the responsibility is greater again. You can't do the things some of your team-mates are doing. Yes, I had to make more sacrifices, but any sacrifice in the world is worth it when you are the captain of Liverpool Football Club, the club you love. I learnt an awful lot by being made captain so young. I grew up.

People think I am a quiet captain, but I don't see it like that. It is just that I would never ever stitch one of my team-mates up in front of the media or the public. What image is it going to create if I start shouting at a young kid in front of 40,000 fans or in front of 25 members of the press, who are then going to write about it?

Of course, there are times in matches when the cameras or the fans will catch me shouting at someone. And my team-mates shout at me, believe me. That is all acceptable. Sometimes the player next to you needs shouting at to tell them they have done something brilliant. Sometimes you need to shout at them to tell them not to make that mistake again. But if you are on someone's back and verbally bullying them, then that is not the right way to lead a team. I won't do that, but have you ever known a Liverpool player to come out and say that I am quiet in the dressing room? That just isn't the case. I prefer to say the right things at the right times. In football, there are plenty of players who make a lot of noise but not much sense comes out of their mouth.

> **My life changed again with the armband on.**

But the most important aspect of being a captain, for me, and I don't care what anyone says, is how you play yourself. It Is not how noisy you are or what you say. It is about what you do. If you are a senior player in the dressing room, then usually the less senior players in there will watch you. That is the most important thing. It is not simply 3 o'clock on a Saturday afternoon when a captain comes into his own. Training that week is just as important and the entire build-up to the game. For example, if the team gets picked on a Thursday and Jay Spearing is playing, I will text him or speak to him and just point out a few things for him to expect in a certain game.

Jay's a great lad. Someone who is still making his way in the game and willing to take on board any advice. I will do it in a quiet way – one-on-one – not wanting people to think I am this noisy captain, roaring in front of people on the Sky cameras. For me, that is the wrong thing to do.

Gerard appointed me because he liked the things that I was doing, but I have learnt from some of the other captains I have played under. I liked Michael Owen's demeanour on the occasions he had the armband on. He was never in your face, ranting and raving, but he preferred to show he was right up for it by going out and scoring a couple. Leading by example.

David Beckham is another captain I hold in high regard. He never said too much in the England dressing room, but when he spoke it was sensible and constructive and, best of all, he went out and performed at a consistent level for the vast majority of his career.

The Armband That Means So Much

My life as a Liverpool player changed for the better on October 15, 2003. That was the first time I was officially Liverpool's captain for a match. We played Olympic Ljubljana in the UEFA Cup at Anfield and won 3-0 with Anthony Le Tallec, Emile Heskey and Harry Kewell scoring. It was a proud, proud day. From that moment on, the way I was viewed and the responsibility I had altered. Team-mates, managers and fans look to the captain to get results and to pull the team through when times are tough. I always prided myself on doing that even without the armband, but now I realised I had to step up another level. I was even more of a role model. It remains one of the best days of my life.

Fully Committed

It is easy to see just how much winning means to players. I'm desperately trying to get the ball on target and the Fulham defenders are doing everything in their power to protect their goal.

Louis Saha is the Fulham player nearest to me and my Liverpool team-mates Emile Heskey and Igor Biscan are looking to get on the end of any ricochets in and around the penalty area. You make a run into the penalty box and 9 times out of 10 you don't get the rub of the green. But you have to keep on going and eventually it will turn for you.

Pass Percentage

I often take risks with my passing. That is just how I play. Nowadays you get statistical analysis of how many passes players attempt, how many are completed and a pass completion percentage.

If I am being honest, I don't take too much notice of them. The figures don't properly differentiate between a pass that I'm trying to squeeze through the eye of a needle and the safe ball an opponent will

play to a team-mate five yards away. I'd rather have a pass completion rate of 73%, but lay on two goals, than make 90% of passes to someone standing within touching distance.

Sheer Joy

My face says it all. There is no better feeling than scoring for your boyhood team and I have been lucky enough to do it quite a bit over the seasons. I think you can see the passion I have for Liverpool here and just what it means to me to score for them. Usually I find myself drawn instinctively towards where the fans are when I find the back of the net. Maybe it's the noise that pulls me towards them, but also I am a fan myself. I would be in with the supporters if I wasn't playing, so to get a result and share it with them is magical.

On the Angle and Goalbound

Another goal against Bolton and another past Jaaskelainen. I possess a decent range in my finishing now. Whether it is shooting from distance, more delicate efforts from close range or scoring with my head, I fancy myself in and around the penalty area. That confidence just comes over time. When you are a kid, you find it tough to stamp your personality on matches because you are worried about making a mistake. Now I am not afraid to miss. Obviously I'm gutted if a gilt-edged chance goes begging, but make no mistake I'll be in there for the next one that comes my way, looking to make amends rather than hiding in the shadows.

Sharing the Moment With Someone Special

Gerard did so much for Liverpool in a short space of time that maintaining those high standards becomes more difficult. Nobody takes into account that other teams improve as well and that the competition to win trophies becomes fiercer. At times, Gerard found himself under pressure and there were the inevitable whispers that he had 'lost the dressing room'. After a left-foot volley at Anfield, I ran over to embrace him by the dug-out. It was a show of support to him to put all the nonsense to bed, which was the least I could do given everything he did for me.

Trying to Clip the Wings of an All Time Legend

You have to appreciate what Ryan Giggs has done in his career. His longevity has apparently been helped by yoga, something I have taken up in recent seasons. Whatever the rivalry between Liverpool and Manchester United, I admire Ryan Giggs so much. To think there was a time in his career when his own supporters were booing him, thinking he had come to the end, is just unbelievable.

Putting on the After Burners

I have 'history' with George Boateng, none of which is his fault. He is playing for Middlesbrough here, but it was while he was at Aston Villa that I was guilty of probably the worst tackle I have ever made in a game. It was a horrible challenge, right by the dug-out. I don't even like speaking about it now. Afterwards, I called him on his mobile to apologise. He was good to me because he could have just slammed the phone down and said he wasn't interested in what I had to say. We had a chat and he just said that he had mistimed a few challenges in his career and added: 'Make sure you learn from this.' The sending-off that day was a turning point for me. I knew I wouldn't make that sort of tackle again.

These Long Limbs Come in Handy

I had my growth spurt when I was 15 and 16. I absolutely shot up in size. Thank goodness I did because without adding a few inches to my frame I honestly don't think I would have played at the top level. I would have had a decent career, but I don't think I would have made it to the very top. Without a doubt my entire career has benefited from me having such long legs.

They mean I can make tackles and do things other players can't, I can reach balls that evade opponents and, generally, they add to my dynamism and help me to get around the pitch effectively. Athleticism is a huge part of the modern-day game and it is becoming more and more important. Look at someone like Cristiano Ronaldo. He is so skilful, but athletic too.

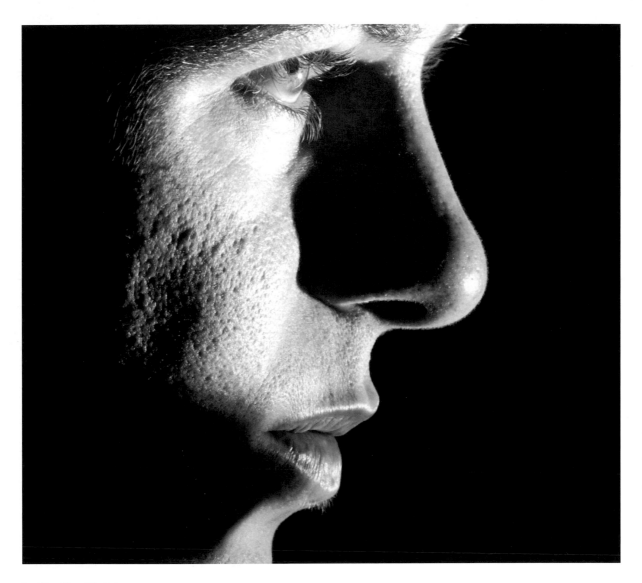

In the Spotlight

My profile has increased over the years as I have achieved more in my career. It is not something that I am totally comfortable with. I'm quite a quiet person, but I understand that it comes with the territory. I know that as captain of Liverpool and now England, I have a responsibility to project myself as a role model and always say and do the right things. Of course that can be hard at times, but the career of a footballer is short and if you are prepared to try to do the right things and make sacrifices the rewards will come. When I was young, Gerard Houllier used to say to all the lads at Liverpool that if we stayed out of nightclubs during our careers, we could own one after we had finished playing. The financial rewards for a Premier League footballer are great, but it has never been about money for me.

CHAPTER 8

2004 — 2005

A SUMMER OF CHANGE

Within weeks of Gerard leaving, at the end of the 2003-04 season, I found my own future being debated on the backs of newspapers and on Sky Sports News. The mobile phone of my agent, Struan Marshall, was on fire that summer with clubs calling him and asking would I be interested in what I always thought would be the unthinkable: leaving Liverpool.

Chelsea, backed by Abramovich's millions and with a new manager in Jose Mourinho at the helm, declared the strongest interest, bidding big money for me, something in the region of £35m. But there was foreign interest as well from the likes of Real Madrid, who were also trying to tempt me away from Anfield.

When you receive those kind of phone calls out of the blue, they are flattering in many respects. It is confirmation that you are doing your job properly and that you are making the most of the talent that you have. It becomes a boost to your confidence when one of the biggest clubs in the world looks and thinks: 'He's a good player. He can make us better.'

If Liverpool had done well in the Premier League that season, I don't think the calls would have come. Clubs knew my bond with Anfield and wouldn't have tried to break that. But when you finish fourth and there is a sense of uncertainty, the vultures circle and look to feast on your insecurities and make the most of the opportunity that is before them.

No one had really called Struan before in my career, but now he had people telling him they'd give me huge pay rises and how great it would be for me to join them. The situation didn't help my performances at Euro 2004 that summer with England. I like to be able to concentrate solely on playing football when I am away with England without any outside interference, but everywhere I went someone wanted to ask me about my future.

In my mind, it was simple. I wanted to stay at Liverpool, but questions needed to be asked. I wouldn't say my head was turned by the interest from elsewhere, but I did want Struan to speak to Liverpool and see what their goals and ambitions were, especially in the aftermath of Gerard leaving. For example, would there be funds available for team strengthening? It was clear that we needed some new blood if we were going to get back to being competitive again.

As much as I love Liverpool, I want to win. I am a footballer and I want to do well in my career and savour as many highs as I can cram in. Of course, I want that to be at Liverpool, but if they could not offer me the reassurances that I was looking for then you naturally think about the future. Thankfully, the answers I wanted were forthcoming and in order to clarify my future I held a press conference at Anfield saying that I would be staying and leading the quest for new trophies.

It was a weight off my mind. I was 24 at the time, my first daughter, Lilly-Ella, had been born in the February of that year and I had moved to the outskirts of Liverpool.

I was settled off the pitch and to uproot everyone, and everything, would have been a huge commitment. There was also the fact that I had only been the captain of Liverpool for one year to take into consideration. Why throw all that away?

Being honest, there have been times since when I thought harder about leaving. Chelsea renewed their interest in me a year later, while the prospect of playing abroad has crossed my mind on a few occasions, more so at the ages of 28-30.

If I ever did leave England, and I can't see it happening now, then Spain would have been my destination. I watch the La Liga games on television when I can and there is something about the football there that appeals to me. Barcelona have made contact in the past. There have been a few phone calls to check what the situation is with me, whether I am happy or not at Liverpool, but there has never been any concrete interest from them.

When Malaga were taken over by backers from Qatar a couple of years ago, they also sounded me out. They wanted to know whether I would be willing to sign up for their project and offered me all sorts of riches.

> **" In my mind, it was simple. I wanted to stay at Liverpool, but questions needed to be asked. "**

More recently Bayern Munich and Paris St Germain have also made it known that they were interested in signing me.

Yet the strongest interest from Spain has always come from Real Madrid, who were keen to take me to the Bernabeu. When you see the stands in that stadium towering towards the heavens it is awe-inspiring and Real are one of the biggest, if not *the* biggest, clubs in the world.

Back in 2004, they did raid Liverpool. It was for Michael Owen rather than me. Losing Michael was a huge blow for the club and also on a personel level. He was someone I had played alongside since we were kids at the Vernon Sangster Sports Centre just setting out on our careers. I knew his runs, exactly where he wanted the ball and I knew he was a player we would find hard to replace. Michael had one year on his contract and was more impatient than me for change. He wanted to get on in his career and found the lure of Real too hard to turn down.

As it was, I was starting to see things from a Spanish perspective as well. But in order to do so I didn't need to leave Liverpool. It was all about the man who had taken over at Anfield and who I hoped was going to take us to the next level. That man was Rafa Benitez.

HOLA, SIGNOR BENITEZ

Within half an hour of meeting Rafa Benitez for the first time, it became apparent that Liverpool would be doing things differently from now on and that I would have to get used to some changes as well.

Gerard Houllier is a man-manager. Someone who loves his players, supports his players, embraces them and wants them to be close to him. Rafa was the opposite.

After being appointed by Liverpool, he requested a meeting with myself, Jamie Carragher and Michael Owen when we were out at Euro 2004 in Portugal. We met him one Friday night at the team hotel and straight away you could notice the difference. He was hands-off and there was going to be a bit of distance between the players and the manager. It didn't matter who you were, a big player or just starting out, the team was all-important. Everyone had to pull in the same direction.

Perhaps that approach is exactly what I needed at that stage of my career, but when you are used to the love and a bit of TLC the change in emphasis was hard for me to accept at first. As it went on, I quite liked the fact that Rafa kept his cards close to his chest and didn't involve me in things as much as Gerard had. I wondered what he thought of me and, as a result of that, it drove me on to impress in every training session and in every game. I wanted him to turn round and embrace me and I thought the breakthrough would come and we would grow close – that a close relationship between the manager and the captain would develop over time. It didn't happen – though not in a bad way, and that's fine.

I had a successful time under Rafa and as you get older you realise football isn't about friends. It isn't about being loved. It isn't about everyone being nice to you. If the manager is distant and does things a different way from the manager before, but we are successful, then bring it on. I'm cool about that. If a manager doesn't speak to me for four years but we win five or six trophies, I will happily take that over a manager who speaks to me every day but under whom we win nothing. It is about results. And I was sure we could get them under Rafa.

Liverpool had played his former club Valencia a couple of times in the Champions League and I liked their style. They were well organised, but played good football at the same time. I also liked the way Rafa looked on the sidelines. I like managers in suits and when they are out in the technical area trying to give instructions and influence the game. I just think it looks good and it offers a sense of reassurance to the players if a game isn't going well.

Gerard had looked to France for a lot of his signings and despite leaving had put in place a deal for us to sign Djibril Cisse, who had scored lots of goals for Auxerre and who would now become even more important given Michael's departure.

Understandably, Rafa turned to the Spanish market he knew well and signed Luis Garcia, Xabi Alonso and Josemi. Antonio Nunez came as part of the deal that took Michael to Real Madrid. Straight away I could see that Xabi had a touch of class about him. His passing range was great, but he was tough as well. He would have no problems settling into English football.

Luis was someone who could inspire one minute and frustrate the next, but he scored some important goals for us. Given the amount of changes that took a hold in the first months of the season – Cisse also broke his leg – it was perhaps no wonder that our form in the Premier League was inconsistent.

In a one-off game we were a match for anyone and that revealed itself in the cup competitions. We reached the Carling Cup Final against Chelsea in Cardiff and while it is an occasion I would rather forget it is one that will live with me forever. For all the wrong reasons.

Given that Chelsea had tried to sign me the previous summer, this was a game that had an extra edge to it even without the fact there was a trophy at stake as well. Then there was Jose Mourinho who had started to wind up the Liverpool supporters during the game by putting his finger to his lips and 'sssh-ing' them. It was a final that none of us wanted to lose. We had started well with John Arne Riise scoring early on and were minutes from getting our hands on the Cup when I looked to clear a free-kick that had been pumped into our penalty area. Instead of heading the ball away, it skimmed the top of my head and flew into the back of our net.

Devastation. Total numbness. This. Cannot. Be. Happening. In that split-second the momentum of the match changed. Chelsea forged ahead in extra time and to compound my misery I was millimetres from getting an equaliser. The ball was played across the box and it just passed by in front of my toe. When the final whistle sounded and Chelsea's players celebrated a 3-2 win, I have never had a worse moment in football.

I held my hand up in the dressing room straight away afterwards and my team-mates rallied round, but it was a long journey home and a long, long night.

You feel sorry for yourself, you sulk, you walk through the door at home and feel totally alone and that's when you want everyone to fuss you.

The disappointment will never vanish and it still hurts talking about that moment all these years on. When I think of myself going up for that header and slightly mistiming my jump, a shiver goes down my spine. I was gutted for a long time after that game, but you cannot hide away. We lost on a Sunday, but by Monday night I knew I had to start fighting again.

There were a lot of fans at Cardiff's Millennium Stadium that day who went home realising that it was an accident. But there were also Liverpool fans in the ground who, given the link with Chelsea, saw my own goal as some sort of grand conspiracy and gave me the height of abuse.

I know because members of my family were in the crowd and were forced to listen to the vitriol. Driving into our training ground at Melwood in the aftermath I knew I couldn't change the past, but I also knew I could make amends in the future.

Redemption proved to be around the corner.

> **It is about results. And I was sure we could get them under Rafa.**

Putting the Laces Through the Ball

The red boots I'm wearing are a rarity because I prefer standard black boots. I don't like putting any undue pressure on myself by having all fancy colours.But they didn't let me down with this free-kick which flew past Portsmouth's Jamie Ashdown in front of the Kop. I've always been willing to step forward and take a free-kick. The confidence

to do so comes from having the
captain's armband on, the trust of
my team-mates and also not being
scared to take criticism if the ball flies
20 yards over the crossbar.

I'll Eat My Shirt!

Although I've been guilty of kissing
the badge before, I don't like seeing
players do it – especially when they
have done it at other clubs, too.
This is a variation I have tried once
or twice. On this occasion it was after
scoring a free-kick against Everton.
I suppose I'm just trying to show how
much playing for Liverpool means
to me. John Arne Riise looks like
he is about to smother me. He is a
great friend and was a really good
player for Liverpool. I think we found
it difficult to replace him when he
left in 2008. He's a player with great
energy, great athleticism and is
excellent on the ball. It was John's
cross that led to my header against
AC Milan in Istanbul.

Power Play

The fact that I am so off-balance demonstrates the power that I have tried to put into this free-kick. Fortunately, it found the back of the net. Unfortunately, we lost the game 3-1 and it proved no more than a consolation strike. The players in the wall tell you how difficult the game was: Pires, Vieira, Gilberto, Van Persie and Fabregas.

Applauding the Twelfth Man

Win, lose or draw, I always clap the fans after every game. Every player should do that as a matter of course. It is a mark of respect for the effort they have made to follow the team. As captain, I wouldn't say to my team-mates, 'Go and clap the fans.' Every player has their own responsibility to do that, but it is something I take seriously.
The Liverpool fans are the best around and that is not just me being biased. Look at some of the people who have said nice things about our supporters, people who have no ties with the club. They have just felt the power of Liverpool fans in full cry and it is an amazing experience.

THE CHAMPIONS LEAGUE ODYSSEY

I have walked out at the Nou Camp with almost 100,000 Catalans whistling at me, played in front of 90,000 fans at Wembley and faced up to the abuse 75,000 supporters inside Old Trafford can muster. Anfield has a capacity of half of some of those venues, but its power remains untouchable. Liverpool's Champions League win in 2005 will forever be synonymous with Istanbul, but do not under-estimate the importance of the raw energy and electricity Anfield conjured up during that rollercoaster run to the final.

If the truth is told, we were maybe only the 10th or 11th best team in Europe that season. But in a game played over two legs, we were up there, and that was overwhelmingly due to the force Anfield exudes. On a big European night, when the stakes are high, there is something in the air in the stadium. It is hard to describe what it is. You can't see it, but you feel it.

It makes the team walking out of the home dressing room feel 10 feet tall and our opponents shrink in size. The tidal wave of momentum the Kop and the other stands generate was first seen against Olympiakos in the group stage when we were cornered and, at half-time, staring elimination full in the face.

When you get a taste for the Champions League, you want to play in it again and again. I hate sitting at home on a Tuesday or Wednesday evening watching the best teams in Europe go at it hammer and tongs, knowing that I am just a helpless spectator.

Our league form had been patchy which meant Europe took on even greater importance for us and I remember doing the press conference the day before the game. We knew we had to beat Olympiakos by two clear goals to progress and I was asked what would happen if we went out of the competition. I answered the question honestly and said I would look at where I felt the club was going, that I would assess things.

I didn't mean 'if we lose, I'm off', but that is how it was interpreted and I can understand why. I was probably a bit rash in what I said and that is one of the press conferences I have learnt the most from.

The next morning, the morning of the game, it was headline news. Seeing my name across the back pages comes with the territory of playing for Liverpool and England. Most interviews I do end up being strongly projected. But I was concerned that the fans would read the headlines and think that if we were beaten I would be definitely leaving. The pressure had been turned up a notch.

The best way of clearing everything up was to make sure we won, but when Rivaldo scored a free-kick midway through the first half we were up against it. That was to be a scenario that brought the best out of us that season and Anfield came alive when we jogged back out for the second-half, needing to score three goals.

Take nothing away from the substitutions Rafa made at the break for getting us over the line though. Florent Sinama Pongolle came on at half-time and Neil Mellor later on, and without their intervention Istanbul would have forever remained a pipe-dream. Make no mistake about that.

Substitutions change games but I must admit that when they both came on, I didn't really see what Rafa was hoping to do. With all due respect to Mellor and Pongolle, they hadn't done a great deal for Liverpool up to that point and they weren't used to playing in games with so much riding on them. Yet within minutes Pongolle scored and then Mellor scrambled a second with nine minutes left to set up a grandstand finish.

One goal. We needed one more goal. I knew the moment would come. All the hours you spend on the training pitch, the times you stay behind and practise after the main session is finished, are for moments like the one that fell to me in the 86th minute that night. Mellor's header set me up perfectly and I knew as soon as I hit a shot from 25 yards that it was going to go close. The shot was going away from the goalkeeper and it found the back of the net. Pandemonium. Then Exhilaration. Then relief.

It is one of my best goals and the funny thing about that is that I never actually felt it. The ball came off my boot so sweetly that it belied the power that I managed to get into the finish. It is a bit like hitting a golf shot when you connect with the ball just right and you don't feel it, there's hardly a reverberation up the club.

We were through, but it was only later in the competition that the players started to get a feeling that this was going to be our year. We had cleared a hurdle, played well, it had been a great night, but at the same time I thought how did we get in that much trouble in the first place?

Beating Juventus over two legs in the quarter-final fuelled the belief in the dressing room and then came Chelsea. Again.

Three months after the lowest point of my career, here was a chance to try and make amends by reaching the Champions League Final.

Chelsea had all the power and strength. They were on their way to winning the title in Mourinho's first season and resembled a relentless machine under him. No one gave us a chance. Drawing 0-0 at Stamford Bridge in the first-leg was a good result, but offered Chelsea as much encouragement as us given away goals counted double.

> **"**
> **Pandemonium.**
> **Then exhilaration.**
> **Then relief.**
> **"**

It was imperative we got off to a good start. Usually when you come out to warm up at Anfield 45 minutes before kick-off, the stands are still quite empty.

That night it seemed every Liverpool supporter realised what was at stake and turned up early on purpose. The noise was deafening. Inspiring every player in red, but intimidating everyone in blue. How could we let them down?

Luis Garcia's happy knack of coming up with big goals was never more crucial than on that night. Chelsea can debate whether the ball crossed the line or not, but consistently overlook that Petr Cech clattered Milan Baros before the rebound fell to Luis and he could have given away a penalty and been sent off. The fact that Luis was in the right place at the right time was no accident. Rafa always worked on the wide players running into the space between opposing full-backs and central defenders and so many goals originate from that move.

Over the two legs, I actually thought Chelsea were a stronger team than us. But we pulled through because we were all in it together. We had our brilliant fans, who created a wall of noise the like of which I had never heard before, and we had some majestic performances.

Sometimes you can win a big game by not necessarily playing great football and playing teams off the park. When it is not going well, you can get through by hanging in there, believing and grabbing the little bits of luck when they come.

We did that against Chelsea and were soon to call upon that blueprint once again.

The Tide Turns in Our Favour

The goal I scored against Olympiakos in the group stages of the Champions League in 2004 is one of my favourites. Everything was against us when Rivaldo curled home a free-kick for the Greek side in the first half, leaving us needing to find three goals in order to progress. Florent Sinama Pongolle and Neil Mellor reduced the arrears before I struck from distance with time running out. I caught the shot so sweetly that as soon as it left my right boot I knew there was a good chance of it hitting the back of the net. I was showered with plaudits afterwards, but without the efforts of Pongolle and Mellor and the rest of the team, the game would have gone long before I got involved.

THAT EPIC FINAL

Istanbul. The very mention of the word makes me smile and brings memories, glorious, surreal memories, flooding back.

The pressure to win silverware at Liverpool is massive. From the moment you sign for the club, you are aware of the history and when you play for the first team that pressure intensifies. So to deliver the biggest trophy in club football when no one expected it was huge.

The night before the final, I couldn't sleep. I get really excited about big games and finals and I was constantly tossing and turning. I couldn't sleep in the afternoon on the day of the game either. Nowadays, I can have 40 winks after training no problem, but that probably has something to do with having three kids and trying to catch up on all the sleep I've missed!

As a result, I found myself yawning and feeling drained when we were doing all our pre-match stuff. It took a while for the adrenaline to kick back in and in many ways that was the same for everyone. We were caught napping as a team when the game started. Instead of realising our dreams, we found ourselves initially plunged into a nightmare.

AC Milan were a strong team with outstanding players, but we made them look exceptional as well. We couldn't get near them.

Paolo Maldini scored inside a minute and, with Kaka running the midfield, the Italians added a second and then a third through goals from Hernan Crespo. Walking off at half-time, I felt embarrassed. We were being humiliated on our big night. We had been played off the park. It was men against boys.

A lot has been said about Rafa's half-time team talk at the Ataturk Stadium, but there was no real mystique to it. He spoke about playing for pride, he mentioned the fans, who had forked out such enormous sums of money to take over Istanbul and the stadium itself, and he urged us to keep believing. 'Let's try and score the next goal,' he said. 'Then, we will see.' Then he ran through the tactical changes, he wanted to implement. Steven Finnan was struggling with an injury and Didi Hamann came on. Rafa wanted me to play a little further forward as a result.

I tried to gee the lads up as well, but at that stage I was simply trying to be positive. Privately, I thought the game was over and I was praying that we would not slip any further behind. 'Please don't let it get to five or six-nil,' I thought.

I cannot fully explain what happened next. Why a game that was beyond us was turned on its head. Yes, we had our togetherness and spirit and Rafa's tactics worked, but you would have to ask AC Milan why they collapsed so dramatically. Why for six minutes at the start of the second half they were so open, so weak and seemed physically tired when they had been like lions before that. It didn't feel like we were playing the same side.

We were different as well. I have scored more eye-catching goals, but the header that flew into the top corner past Dida from John Arne Riise's cross is undoubtedly the most important of my entire career. It offered us a foothold and more importantly gave us a slither of hope.

From the dressing room at half-time we had all heard 'You'll Never Walk Alone' echo around the arena. It was sung in open defiance. Now the noise from the stands carried more belief. Could we do it? When Vladimir Smicer scored from distance moments later, the Ataturk erupted. The great escape was on.

Milan Baros was often criticised for not having a great sense of awareness for what was happening on the pitch, but the little touch he played into my path as we sought the equaliser was exquisite. An arm in my back from Gennaro Gattuso and I was sent sprawling. Penalty. Xabi Alonso stepped up to take the spot-kick and although Dida saved his effort, he smashed home the rebound into the roof of the net. Amazing.

We had all been scooped up and swept along in a whirlwind, but there was no chance to consider what we had just done. As soon as the scoreline went to 3-3, I was thinking 'penalties. Let's get to penalties.'

The shock of throwing away such a commanding advantage seemed to stir Milan to their senses, like a boxer being givien smelling salts. They poured forward again.

We dug in, putting our bodies on the line and then relying on a bit of luck as well. Jamie Carragher was immense in defence – defying Milan time after time as well as the cramp that was shooting up his legs – and then there was Jerzy Dudek.

Talk to him today and he still does not know how he managed to save a header from Andrei Shevchenko that looked goal-bound. The look of disbelief on Shevchenko's face immediately afterwards is priceless.

In that split second, Milan had it confirmed to them that this was not going to be their night and their lack of confidence was evident in the penalty shoot-out that followed.

Didi, Vladi and Djibril Cisse scored for us and even though Riise was wayward, Milan could not afford another miss from 12 yards.

Rafa had put me down to take the fifth penalty that night which, given the misses before from Milan, had the potential to be the crucial spot-kick. No problem. I was up for it. But when people say, 'Oh, you are so lucky to be a footballer' and 'I would give anything to be a footballer, you have such an easy life and get paid all this money' they have to remember the flipside. What I say to those people is straightforward. Could you handle the pressure of knowing that you are five seconds away from taking a penalty in the Champions League Final? And not only that, but you are five seconds away from taking the penalty that could win the Champions League for Liverpool? Do you fancy that? Could you cope with that, knowing that if you miss you could be remembered for that for the rest of your life?

So when Shevchenko was walking up to take the penalty that Milan needed to score to ensure I would have to step into the spotlight, that is what I was thinking. I was preparing myself rather than watching what was happening. I was confident of scoring and I was going to place my effort rather than going for power.

> **"**
> **I felt embarrassed. We were being humiliated.**
> **"**

In a pressure situation like the one Shevchenko was under, the last thing I thought was that he was going to dink his spot-kick.

So when Jerzy pulled off the save, it was a split second before I realised I wouldn't have to take my penalty after all and that we had won the Champions League, or the European Cup as it was before, for a fifth time.

And then it hit me. I was off. Off trying to catch Carra, off to celebrate with my team and our fans.

The celebrations went on into the early hours of the morning. There was no time to sleep. Each and every one of us was too caught up in what we had just achieved. Relief and euphoria were my over-riding emotions and then I felt drained and tired for days after because the pressure in the build-up and during the game itself was intense. But to have 'Champions League winner' on my CV, well, it doesn't get any better than that.

The trophy we won is on display in reception at the training ground and I walk past it every day. When I see it, or when I am watching a Champions League game at home, moments from that match against Milan flash into my mind. But I don't really reflect on and wallow in that triumph much any more. I will never forget that night, but it no longer feels fresh. These days, I think more about what else I can win before I finish my career; what other trophies I can lift before I call it a day.

Shock and Awe

This picture tells a thousand words. We're all shell-shocked as we wait for AC Milan to kick off following another goal in Istanbul. If you look at my face I'm thinking, 'They're too good for us. We're not going to win this game. We're getting the runaround.' How often have you seen Xabi Alonso in the last few years look like that, just staring in the distance, helpless? It doesn't happen to him, does it? You can shout and try to coax some belief back into your team-mates, but it is hard to make yourself heard in that sort of atmosphere. Also, it is tough to say anything meaningful that isn't just trying to paper over the cracks. We were 3-0 down at half-time and surely down and out.

Coming to Terms With a Disastrous First Half

Knowing Rafa, he is probably telling me to get control of Kaka and get someone on Andrea Pirlo. And knowing me, I'm probably saying, 'It's impossible.' We were getting over-run so much in midfield it was a nightmare. Pirlo earned rave reviews at Euro 2012 for the way he played for Italy, especially in the penalty shoot-out win over England in the quarter-finals. If you give him time and space, he will look good because technically, with the ball at his feet, he is as good as anyone in the world. If you get bodies around him, you can run off him and I don't think he is very physical but he controls games with his passing if you let him.

Heading in the Right Direction

I have scored better goals and come up with more eye-catching strikes, but, without doubt, this is the most important goal-scoring intervention of my entire career. It gave us back a little bit of respect, and some belief too, but I still didn't think it would spark the tremendous fight-back that followed. I checked my initial run because John Arne Riise's first cross was blocked, then I gambled on going into the box again. What is surprising about the goal when you see this picture is how much space I had between Jaap Stam and Alessandro Nesta, who were two of the best defenders in the world at the time. To get a header right in the middle of them, and in a game of that magnitude, was special for me. The header was instinctive. I went for accuracy rather than power because the cross was that good.

If the Fans Believe It, So Will We

At half-time at the Ataturk Stadium we were despondent in the dressing room but we could hear the strains of 'You'll Never Walk Alone' being sung by the Liverpool supporters outside. On the way back to the half-way line after my goal, I waved my hands towards the fans to show that the players were with them and that we hadn't given up either. They had descended on Istanbul in their thousands and the very least they deserved was for us to keep going. They responded to my gesture by creating even more of a din, but that's the Liverpool fans for you. The best in the world.

Turning Point

Vladimir Smicer had just scored from distance and the momentum was now with us when I screamed at Milan Baros to nudge the ball into my path as I looked to burst into the area. His touch was perfect and Gennaro Gattuso put a hand on my back, pushed me off balance and sent me crashing to the floor. Penalty. I wanted to take the spot-kick and for a large part of that season I was our designated penalty taker.
But Rafa had a thing where he named a different penalty taker for different games and he would go off his head – shouting and fining players – if someone disobeyed his orders. He named Xabi as the penalty taker for the final before the game and while I was personally gutted, I knew Xabi was deadly. OK, Dida saved his first attempt but when he fired the rebound into the roof of the net our comeback was complete. 3-3. Amazing.

I've Done It For You

Here I'm blowing a kiss to my family who were in the crowd. My dad and brother were among a gang of friends who had travelled to Turkey for the game and this was for them. The drama of our penalty shoot-out win gave way to the best celebrations I have ever known and I wanted my family to be a part of it. I owe everything to them, for the support they have given me over the years and the belief they have always had in me. I'm proud to have given them something back. The red wristband I am wearing is in support of the Hillsborough Family Support Group.

Champions at Last

The scene still takes my breath
away. Sometimes I sit and think:
'How did that team win that trophy?'
We had six or seven players who
were up there with the best in
Europe, but without being
disrespectful to anyone else, there
were others who were not quite
as good. I knew straight away what
a massive achievement this was.
It was the best night of my life and
I doubt it will ever be bettered.
With the amount of money that is
in football now with the likes of
Chelsea, Manchester City,
Paris St Germain and Real Madrid,
it is going to get a lot harder for
Liverpool to win this trophy again.
Not least because it is a lot harder
for Liverpool to even qualify for the
Champions League nowadays.

Happy Scousers

I have grown close to Jamie Carragher in recent years, probably since Michael Owen and Danny Murphy both left the club in the summer of 2004. We share a room together on away trips and as captain and vice-captain we feel a lot of responsibility on us. He was magnificent in Istanbul, defying cramp, putting his body on the line, repelling wave after wave of attacks from Milan after we had come back to 3-3. For two homegrown lads to stand shoulder to shoulder on one of the best nights in the club's history is special. Carra is a Liverpool legend and a good friend.

Planting a Smacker on the Trophy

Alex, my wife, says I kissed that Cup more than her. After the joy came relief. I had grown up knowing what European football meant to Liverpool Football Club. I had seen the tapes of Emlyn Hughes, Phil Thompson and Graeme Souness lifting the European Cup and I wanted that for myself. I wanted to deliver that trophy for all the Liverpool fans out there.

The Red Sea

You could feel the bus literally rocking as we snaked our way through Liverpool City Centre the night after Istanbul. Police horses were banging into the bus as they tried to hold the fans back. It was mayhem, but glorious, brilliant mayhem. I just don't think you would see this scene anywhere else in the world. When have you ever seen that before? It is a majestic sight. Wow. Mind-blowing. We crawled through the streets of Liverpool and every player on that bus took away memories that they will never ever forget. Afterwards, we had a party in town. That was a late night!

CHAPTER 9

2005
—
2006

UP FOR THE CUP AGAIN

Just 49 days after our season had gloriously ended, and with the miracle of Istanbul still uppermost in everyone's thoughts, we stepped back out onto a football pitch again.

No one at Liverpool could complain too much. UEFA had ripped up their own rule book to allow us to defend our Champions League trophy because we had finished fifth in the Premier League and outside of the criteria for entry into Europe's élite. Not allowing the Champions League winners back into the competition would have defied logic and the morning after our win over AC Milan, the pressure began to snowball on the authorities until they had no option but to cave in. So stepping out against Welsh part-timers Total Network Solutions (TNS) at Anfield on 13 July did not seem like a hardship.

On a personal note, I started the campaign as I meant to go on. I grabbed a hat-trick against TNS that night and in total scored seven goals in my first four games of the season.

I was up and running, my confidence pepped by what had happened in Istanbul, and I finished the campaign with 23 goals, which was by far the best goals return of my career up to that point.

Collectively, Liverpool were much more competitive as well. Our Champions League success had masked what had been a disappointing Premier League campaign and we couldn't rely on conquering Europe every season. Something had to change.

One of Rafa's great strengths around this time was that he would never make the same mistake twice.

Liverpool weren't physically strong enough the season before so he rectified that in the transfer market. The revolving door at Anfield spun faster than I had known. In came Pepe Reina, Momo Sissoko, Peter Crouch and Bolo Zenden along with others. Out went Milan Baros, Antonio Nunez and Mauricio Pellegrino. It didn't matter that Jerzy Dudek had been one of the heroes of Istanbul. Rafa felt the goalkeeping position needed strengthening and even before the Champions League Final he had lined up a deal for Reina. You have to say that was one of his best transfers. Baros, too, had played his part in one of the greatest nights in Liverpool's history. But there is no sentiment in football. He left to make room for Crouch.

The pressure to perform at Liverpool is always intense. We drew four of our first five Premier League games, and then lost 4-1 at home to Chelsea, and you could sense people were sharpening their knives to plunge into Rafa. The criticism lingered on the assumption that he couldn't get to grips with the unique features of English football, the pace, intensity and physical nature of the game here.

Rubbish. And we soon exposed that myth. When we beat West Ham at home on 29 October, the win didn't feel out of the ordinary. It was routine. Yet it acted as a springboard for us to go on an exceptional run of form. We won 10 straight games in the league and when James Beattie scored a consolation for Everton in a 3-1 win at Goodison Park in December, it was the first time Pepe had conceded a goal in the league for almost two months.

There are times when, as a team, you play almost on auto-pilot. That stems from the trust you have in your team-mates. We had the best goalkeeper in the world In Pepe and two of the best defenders in the world in Carra and Sami. I was being given licence to roam from the right of midfield and we had Xabi and Momo who were ruthlessly efficient. Plus, we had lots of players who could chip in with goals: Riise, Fernando Morientes, Crouchy, Luis Garcia, Zenden and Harry Kewell.

We weren't the finished article by any stretch of the imagination, but we weren't the pushovers we had been on too many occasions the previous season, that was for sure. Football is all about making progress.

There was a disappointment during that purple patch, but it came on foreign soil. We had travelled to Japan just before Christmas for the World Club Championship by virtue of our Champions League success.

To be crowned the best team on the planet was a huge incentive for us, more so because the great Liverpool teams of the past had always failed to get their hands on the trophy. How we came up short I don't know. We battered Brazilian side Sao Paulo in the final, seeing goals dubiously disallowed, but still lost 1-0. Rafa was fuming afterwards, but the season would contain a silver lining.

> **The pressure to perform at Liverpool is always intense.**

We had gone out of the Carling Cup in a shock defeat to Crystal Palace and been dumped out of the Champions League by Benfica, losing both legs, but the FA Cup provided us with a great source of satisfaction. En route to the final we beat Manchester United in the fifth round and Chelsea in the semi-finals, so no one could accuse us of having an easy draw. Of course, the final itself turned into a drama with the penalty shoot-out win over West Ham, but there was a sense of accomplishment at the end of that season.

We were never going to leap from fifth to first in the table, but finishing third with 82 points, one point behind Manchester United and nine points adrift of champions Chelsea showed we were making strides. Making that final step is the most difficult, but there were clues as to how we should go about trying to get there. Of the six games we lost in the league that season, two were against Chelsea and one was against Manchester United.

If we could correct that imbalance, Liverpool would become genuine contenders. I finished the season positive about the future. I believed that under Rafa, Liverpool were becoming a force again.

An Unsung Hero

Pako Ayesteran's role in the success Liverpool enjoyed under Rafa Benitez often gets overlooked. He was Rafa's assistant, the link between the players and the manager, as well as being an innovative coach.

All the trophies we won in that period came while Pako was alongside Rafa in the dug-out and I often wonder what he could have achieved had he stayed, instead of leaving at the start of the 2007-08 season.

In Rafa We Trust

Rafa Benitez pushed me more than any other manager I have had in my career and, at the time he came to Liverpool, I needed that. He didn't ever give out any credit, but he made me a better, more rounded player who could play in a variety of positions and appreciate what being a team player was all about. At times we didn't always see eye-to-eye, and I will never forgive him for substituting me against Everton at Goodison Park in 2007. Lucas, who replaced me, earned the penalty that enabled us to win 2-1, but I felt the decision was disrespectful because I was playing well.

On the Spot

I always fancy my chances from the penalty spot. Over the years I think I have a good record. Up to the end of last season, I had taken 34 and scored 27. Five have been saved and twice I have missed the target. The key is to know exactly where you are going to put the ball. If the goalkeeper pulls off a great save then sometimes there is nothing you can do about it other than to say, 'well done'. The worst thing is changing your mind in your run-up and that has cost me in the past. Nowadays I go for placement rather than power. But if I miss, I'll be back ready to take the next one.

The Best Fans in Football

Having stood on the Kop as a kid, I know what the supporters think, how they feel and what they expect from someone in a red shirt. They want 100% commitment first of all and if you offer that you find they'll support you through anything. The first time they sung my name, I was taken aback – they can't really be singing about me, can they? It remains one of the best experiences I've had as a player: the fans chanting my name and being totally behind me.

Best Seat in the House

Being able to put a smile on the faces of these supporters is one of the reasons I play football. It is an amazing feeling to know that you are only ever a couple of seconds away from lighting up the stadium and transforming the mood among 40,000 fans. Supporters can feel alienated in this day and age, but I'll always try to do as much as I can for them. If celebrating a goal in front of them makes them feel good then that is great.

He's Giving Me Twisted Blood

There are a handful of players who I have played with or against who are on a different planet from the majority of players in the Premier League. Cristiano Ronaldo is one of them. He is a freak (I mean that as a compliment!); he is unique. He has raised the bar in terms of skill, constantly pushing himself to stay one step ahead of the defenders who gang up on him, trying to stop him. There are not many players that you genuinely worry about facing, but Ronaldo is one of them because he can win a game on his own. He showed that at Manchester United and is now doing it game in and game out at Real Madrid. I love watching him. He takes my breath away.

Precision Placement

Set-pieces have a huge part to play In the modern game and that is why getting the delivery right is so important. There is nothing more frustrating than seeing a corner hit the first defender or fly over the head of everyone in the penalty area. Having said that, you can have great delivery but if you haven't got the players in the team who are prepared to finish the job off then that is no use either. This is where you need your team-mates to be brave. If you haven't got players who are prepared to break their nose or their jaw, or get their face mangled, in order to smash a header into the back of the net, then there is no point in putting the ball on a sixpence.

What Will They Ask Me Next?

Dealing with the media and attending press conferences is part of a player's job. I understand how important the media is in the modern game and I try to be as honest as I can when I am answering questions. Sometimes it has got me into trouble in the past and people have said I am too honest, but that is hardly a fault is it? The manager has a weekly press conference at Melwood in the build-up to games, and the players are asked to stop and talk to the press after matches. I am in the papers and on TV quite a lot so I tend to limit what I do during the season, but it is a responsibility I take seriously.

Losing Never Gets Any Easier

There is a common misconception about my career that it has always been on an upward curve. There have been plenty of highs, but several lows as well, which act as a kick in the stomach and never get any easier to take. I once read Ryan Giggs say that he lingers on the defeats in his career longer than the triumphs and I know what he means. Losing the FIFA Club World Championship to Brazilian side Sao Paulo 1-0 in Yokohama in 2005 was a major blow that often gets overlooked now. How we didn't win, I don't know. We had three goals disallowed and it felt as if the officials were against us. We would have made history had we won because no Liverpool team had ever lifted that trophy. When the moment passed by, I was left alone with my thoughts. The only consolation is that not many players get the chance to play in a game like this.

A Huge Honour

I would like to think that over the years I have proved myself to be a team player. Liverpool comes first, my team-mates come first. Individual awards, of course, are nice, the icing on the cake. To be voted PFA Players' Player of the Year in 2006 was a great honour because it meant I had the respect of not just my team-mates, but players up and down the country. I scored 23 goals that season for Liverpool and felt as good as I have ever felt walking onto a pitch. Give me the Premier League title that season, however, and I would have gladly handed the Player of the Year trophy back.

It's There!

Complacency undermines everything you do as a footballer and makes life harder. We almost found that to our cost in the FA Cup Final in 2006 against West Ham. To be honest, I thought we just had to turn up and wipe the floor with them, winning two, three, four-nil. We were the favourites, the pitch at the Millennium Stadium was huge, surely we would make our superiority tell? Any thought of that was soon banished as they grabbed a two-goal lead to leave Liverpool staring humiliation in the face. Djibril Cisse halved the deficit before the break and I scored the first of my two goals afterwards following a knock-down from Peter Crouch. The ball just sat up nicely for me and I was in the right place at the right time to smash it into the roof of the net. Typically, the drama didn't end there.

Cramp – The Downside of Extra Time

I build myself up so much for the big games that I tend use up a lot of energy before I even kick a ball simply because I want to win so much. I've never been a good sleeper before important matches because it's whirling around my head just what is at stake. Liverpool as a club was fashioned on winning silverware, so every chance you get to make new history you have to take it. Cramp is a consequence of all that. The Millennium Stadium pitch was huge, it was a blazing hot day and for a large part of the game we were chasing round trying to get ourselves back into contention. When cramp takes hold you feel like you are restricted, like your muscles are snapping. It's horrible. It's different, too, from the cramp you sometimes get when you are in bed. Sami Hyypia is on hand here to try and get me going again, bending back my toes in order to freshen my legs up.

Sweet as a Nut

As a one-off shot, I have never connected with a ball better than here. It flew past Shaka Hislop from 35 yards. It really was a boom or bust moment. There were just seconds left before the final whistle and West Ham were still leading 3-2. If I'd had more energy, I would have sought to control the ball and looked to have found a team-mate. As it was, it was all that I could do to whack it. Sometimes they go in, sometimes they don't. You can see the West Ham fans in the background, standing up in their seats, probably praying that it goes a yard wide. I surprised myself because you never expect to score a goal like that in those circumstances.

Taking Responsibility

Even in extra time West Ham gave us a couple of scares, but once we reached penalties I was confident we would come out on top. After Istanbul the previous season, we had experience of the pressure that comes with a shoot-out. I was due to have taken the fifth penalty in the Champions League Final, but ultimately I was not required. Here, I am first up. Rafa Benitez put his trust in me and I always feel I can deliver because I am not afraid to miss. That is the key. Believe in yourself and don't fear what might happen.

Jubilation Reigns

People talk about 'The Steven Gerrard Final' but you can see from this picture it wasn't all about me. Ultimately, we celebrated because of the role Pepe Reina played in the shoot-out. To get another FA Cup winners' medal to add to the one I won in 2001 was brilliant. I really like this photo: Hyypia, Hamann, Finnan, me, Sissoko, Carragher, Morientes, Riise. I trusted these team-mates and it is one of the best Liverpool teams I have played in. We were strong, physical and had a real sense of togetherness.

Rafa, Me and the Pursuit of Trophies

The perfect end to the perfect day. Rafa became the first ever Liverpool manager to win two major trophies in his first two seasons. At the time, it seemed like we would just carry on winning silverware, but unfortunately it didn't work out like that. I think Rafa has respect for me as a player, but I don't think he appreciated how lucky he was to have Carra and me in our prime. Maybe I didn't appreciate fully what being manager of Liverpool is like when you have Chelsea and Manchester United to compete with.

CHAPTER 10

2006
—
2007

DEALING WITH FAME

It is strange the first time someone asks for your autograph. You are a star in the eyes of the person thrusting a pen and a piece of paper at you, yet you are the one who feels awkward and shy initially.

Like everyone does I'd practised my signature lots of times growing up, imagining making the grade for Liverpool, but being in the public eye has never sat easily with me. Even now, I don't really like doing interviews for the media. I try to be honest whenever I do them and I respect the media not only because I know how big and important they are, but only because they have always been respectful to me.

But I am happiest coming into work just to play football: to train and play the game at the weekend. Yet, it is not possible when you are playing in the best league in the world to simply do that. I had noticed that more people had started to take notice of me when I returned from Euro 2000 with England.

Things snowballed from there. Winning the Champions League in the awe-inspiring manner Liverpool did in 2005, the performance I produced in the FA Cup Final in 2006 and then scoring twice for England in the World Cup Finals later that same year simply ensured that my reputation spread.

Reaching a second Champions League Final in three seasons as we did in 2006-07 ensured that the focus was rarely off the club and myself.

Playing and scoring around the world led to camera crews and journalists from Germany, France and Spain wanting to come and interview me.

If I agree to every request that the press department at Liverpool receive, there would be no time to play.

I am not going to deny that when you are younger all the attention you receive is great. You do get a bit big-headed, you do milk it and any player who says they haven't enjoyed a bit of press attention over the years is telling lies.

It's nice to pick up the paper and see someone praising you. In any walk of life people like praise, but it is important to take criticism as well. I have had it drilled into me that you can't linger on any hype or praise. I know when I have played well and deserve plaudits, and I know when I haven't. Over the years I have probably been too hard on myself in interviews and too honest, but I refuse to see that as a negative. My honesty pushes me on and is one of the main reasons I have found a level of consistency over my career.

I only ever get the hump with the media if someone is being unfair, but, equally, I'll take no notice of a piece if they are trying to cosy up to me for no reason. I can read between the lines. I'm not soft. I don't revel in people praising me. I want to be around people who treat me as a normal person.

All the people I am close to – my family, my wife Alex, and my friends – they don't brown nose me or over-praise me. I don't surround myself with people who just say, 'yes, yes, yes'. I am quite selective in who I will allow to get close to me because there are so many slippery slopes to go down as a footballer.

The introduction of camera phones and the explosion of social media mean trust becomes a big issue for players. I would say I have a dozen close friends who are in my life day in, day out and who know a lot of private stuff about me and my family. But I don't want to upset anyone because I'll have a coffee or a bite to eat with plenty more and they are important to me as well.

I have had to adapt. Nowadays I try to create a low profile off the pitch, while trying my best every day in training and in games so as to keep my standards as a footballer high. It is a balancing act.

Part of my appreciation of how best to deal with being in the public eye was shaped by Gary McAllister when he arrived at Liverpool. We are looked after by the same agent, Struan Marshall, and so I knew Gary was coming to Liverpool in 2000. Having played against him before I realised he was someone I could learn from. From the moment he walked into the dressing room Gary has always been someone who was prepared to talk to me. He was one of the people who spoke to me about my tackling in the early days and he helped me to channel my aggression in the right way. Not many people in football have the balls to come and tell you when you have done something wrong. A lot of people just want to talk to you about things you have done right. Gary said it as he saw it and I owe him for that.

> **" I want to be around people who treat me as a normal person. "**

These days I try to take on the role Gary did so well during the time he was at Anfield. I think it is so important for young lads in any team to have older ones around them, players who will offer pointers and advice about the game and the pitfalls away from the pitch. It is priceless. The worry I have is whether the young players want to listen or whether they think you are being 'busy', as we say in the game, which basically means to mither them.

It tells you a lot about the young lads at the club when you see how they react. If their eyes glaze over and they can't wait for you to go, then I take the view that it's their loss and I'm not going to keep on taking time to speak to them if they are not interested.

I'd say the ones who listen, like I did, are the ones who take the advice and tips on board, giving themselves a better chance of succeeding. I can speak to my younger cousin, Anthony Gerrard, who plays for Cardiff City, and some of the things he says to me stick, so the way I look at it is you never stop learning as a footballer.

I'll help anyone at Liverpool and with England too. After all, we are striving for the same thing: success.

Kung Fu Panda

Another test for the groins! No wonder I've had niggles over the years. I'm probably trying to reach, unsuccessfully it would seem, a cross from one of my team-mates. Rather that than my touch being poor.
I think it shows two things. Firstly, the determination I have to go the extra yard for Liverpool Football Club and, secondly, the increasing physical demands that players are placed under. Far more emphasis is put on rehabilitation these days than when I first started. Sport science, with practices such as ice baths, has become a major part of the game. I would say that is the biggest change I have noticed over the years.

Catching My Breath in the Cauldron of Old Trafford

Gary Neville once asked me on an England trip whether I would fancy playing for Manchester United. I just laughed. It is unthinkable. I actually love going to Old Trafford, though. It is a tough, tough venue and you know you are going to have to play well to come away with anything.

Over the years, I've had mixed results there: some good wins and some performances in which we haven't done ourselves justice. Banter from the crowd is part and parcel of football. As long as it doesn't overstep the mark, I have no problem with it.

In the Full Glare

If I could be in charge of the Premier League for one day, I would scrap all lunchtime kick-offs and go down the foreign route of playing games at night. The atmosphere is better, the pitches are always extra slick because of the dew that falls on them, and there is just a better tempo to games that are played under floodlights. I much prefer playing under lights than in daylight. That is the downside of the increasing influence television companies exert on our games. I think Sky has been brilliant for the Premier League, but maybe they could just schedule a few more of our games at 8pm, although I understand they have scheduling commitments around the world.

Upended in Full Flight

He's one dirty hatchet man, that Joe Cole (only joking!). To be fair, I have kicked him a few times so I'll take one back no problem. Joe's very talented, but his enthusiasm for playing football shines through above all else. He had a difficult time at Liverpool when he arrived and wasn't helped by the uncertainty off the pitch. But it says everything about him that he went to Lille in France on loan for a season to play and sample a new culture and that he has come back to try and prove he can be successful in a red shirt.

The Long Walk to Destiny

Penalty shoot-outs have played a big part in my career both with Liverpool and England. You are talking about fine margins, the difference between reaching finals and semi-finals, winning trophies and going home as losers. The second time we played Chelsea in a Champions League semi-final in 2007, the drama was no less than when we met the first time. I will always put my name forward for a shoot-out. If I miss from 12 yards, I'm not one of these players who will say I don't want another one. You have to accept that sometimes the keeper will guess right and pull off a good save, or that your accuracy won't be spot-on all the time. Thankfully, I scored here and overall I am pleased with my penalty record, considering some of the situations I have been in. The walk is long, especially in this

situation, knowing you are trying
to reach a Champions League Final
against a very good team. In fact,
it is too long and you have too long
to think, but that is part of the test.
With a couple of penalties that I
have missed I have changed my
mind on the way to taking them.
So I stick to my plan now. If I go the
way I intend and the keeper saves it,
I accept it.

Rubbing Shoulders With One of the All Time Greats

Paolo Maldini is one of the few players my wife Alex has enjoyed watching over the years! She's quite keen on him, as I suppose all girls are. My respect for Maldini is similar to the respect I have for Ryan Giggs. When you are playing for one of the biggest clubs in the world, in AC Milan, every week for decades, not just years, and playing consistently well, you deserve legendary status.

Don't under-estimate how difficult that is. On the few occasions I have met him, he has come across as a humble man, which is testament to him, given everything he has done.

Kaka Thanks His Maker

There are two sides to any final – joy and despair. Kaka is in ecstasy and I'm distraught. The Brazilian was probably one of the best players in the world around that time. The irony is that both he, and AC Milan, played better in Istanbul than in Athens two years later. That's football.

Contemplating the One That Got Away

The reason why the Champions League Final of 2007 grates with me so much is because it was a missed opportunity. The sort I may not ever get again in my career. The team selection wasn't right that night. In my opinion, there wasn't enough pace in the starting line-up to hurt Milan, plus we gave them two soft goals. If we had been sliced apart, then I would have accepted defeat, however reluctantly. But that night still fills me with regrets.

CHAPTER 11

2007
2008

BOARDROOM POLITICS

Looking back now it feels like I was brainwashed, but at the time I was excited by the plans of Tom Hicks and George Gillett. To compete with the likes of Chelsea, Manchester United and the other mega-forces across Europe (this was before Manchester City became such an important financial powerhouse) you need to be able to buy the best players when they become available.

In the words of David Moores, the Liverpool chairman at the time, he wasn't rich enough to do that. So he sold the club in February 2007 to Hicks and Gillett and I can understand why he felt they were genuine, why he felt they had the best interests of the club at heart. I felt all those things, too.

When I sat down with the two Americans at a meeting in the Lowry Hotel in Manchester, they blew me away, with what they were planning to do and the ideas they had. Me and Jamie Carragher were on England duty for a game against Spain at the time and the coach Steve McClaren said it was OK for the new owners to come over and see us.

Rick Parry, Liverpool's chief executive, brought Hicks and Gillett over to the meeting and, over the course of half an hour, they spoke about ambitious plans for a new stadium in the shadow of Anfield and of backing Rafa in the transfer market. I was happy and to be fair to Hicks and Gillett, they were as good as their word on some things, albeit initially. They had paid for Fernando Torres to come in that summer, but soon after, the storm clouds gathered.

The first time I started to get uneasy was in the autumn of 2007 when rumours started to circulate that Rafa was under pressure. He had given a bizarre press conference in which he kept on repeating the phrase 'coaching and training', in response to a barbed request from Hicks to stop getting involved at all levels of the club and focus on what he was best at – coaching and training. Those were Rafa's strengths, no doubt about it, but he didn't take kindly to an American in cowboy boots telling him that.

Relations became strained from there and the media had a field day as it did throughout the Hicks and Gillett tenure. I have learnt a lot in my career about how the media and the press operates. I understand briefing takes place and when your ears prick up it is usually for a reason. Stories do not come out of nothing and the idea that the club was thinking of sacking Rafa was a concern if not a huge surprise, as he had started clashing with the people above him at the club.

I was equally concerned that Jurgen Klinsmann, the former Germany striker, was the man in the frame to replace Rafa. He had played at Tottenham, but what did he know about managing in English football? At the time, I was thinking, 'We've just reached two Champions League Finals in three years, Rafa is a top manager, why do we even need a change?' If you ask me now: 'Rafa or Klinsmann?' I would say Rafa, all day long.

Yet as a team we found ourselves in a situation where if we didn't beat Marseille in our last Champions League group game, we would have been out of the competition. Rafa? The signs were that he would have been out of a job.

As a team, we were awesome that night. We had worked on our shape so much before that game that I knew we were going to be hard to beat. From the first whistle, we were too strong and too powerful for the French. We were constantly in their faces and swatted them aside 4-1. It was a great display. We were through and Rafa was safe. For now.

But the lull did not last and for two-and-a-half years everything at Liverpool was permanently in a state of flux. The club was being sold. No it wasn't. Rafa was going. No he wasn't. Hicks and Gillett were fighting. Yes they were.

Plans for the stadium had ground to a halt, players were leaving and the money was not being reinvested. In short, it was a nightmare. A constant headache. A worrying shadow was cast over the entire club to the extent that the threat of actually going out of business hung over us. We were front-page news as much as back page. My head was wrecked.

I get angry and frustrated when I think about how Liverpool Football Club lurched towards High Court battles off the pitch and slipped down the Premier League on it.

We were in Spain for a pre-season game against Espanyol in the summer of 2009 when it became clear to me that we were going to struggle. Xabi Alonso had left to join Real Madrid for £30m and the club would not be reinvesting all the money from his departure in the team. The banks needed some of it. At the time, I was thinking there is no player in the world who is going to come in to Liverpool and be as good as Xabi had been, so to then find out that we couldn't use all of the proceeds from his sale was a blow. Alberto Aquilani joined from AS Roma for £18m, but he came with an injury and never really settled. He is a good player, but he's not Xabi.

That night against Espanyol, we were poor. Sometimes in pre-season, you dismiss the result as meaning nothing, given the games are primarily exercises in boosting fitness. But I looked at our squad that night and looked at how other teams were strengthening and I knew we would struggle to finish in the top four that season.

We went out of the Champions League in the group stages and were off the pace in the Premier League once again. We were immersed in a cycle of mediocrity on the field and open warfare between the supporters and the owners off it.

The situation was such that, when you are captain, you think: 'Do I get involved in this or stick to playing?' When you walk out of Anfield 45 minutes after a home game and there are still thousands of supporters in their seats protesting against the owners of the football club it is a desperately sad sight. Liverpool Football Club, as I knew it, felt as if it was slipping away.

No one – certainly not the fans or the players – wanted Hicks and Gillett any more, but they were hanging on to the club for grim death, aware hundreds of millions were riding on whether they could sell it or not.

I knew that was wrong. I knew they needed to go, but I thought long and hard, most days if not every day, about whether me coming out and saying something publicly would help the situation?

I totally understand that people thought, 'Gerrard is the captain. He should come out and say something. He knows what is happening can't go on.' Behind the

> **" Liverpool Football Club, as I knew it, felt as if it was slipping away. "**

scenes me and Jamie Carragher were constantly asking questions and saying this needs to stop, but we are not the type of players to go and do exclusives in papers and add fuel to the fire.

It was a delicate situation. Apart from the fact that it's hard to think of any other workforce around the world coming out and attacking the people who own the institution they work for, I wondered what me slagging off Hicks and Gillett in the national papers or on Sky would have achieved. Would it have brought about a solution any quicker? I don't know for sure, but I doubt it.

There was also the fact that when I was asking questions behind the scenes, people like Rafa and managing director, Christian Purslow, were telling us they were taking care of things. Players can influence matters on the pitch, not in the boardroom.

In the end, I was just relieved that all the mess was cleared up and that the club won its case in the High Court in October 2010, forcing Hicks and Gillett to sell. They had taken Liverpool to the brink, selfishly putting themselves first and willing to risk the longevity of a club that is adored by hundreds of millions of people around the world.

Our most important result of the season came that day, not least because as a player it meant I could focus on playing football again. Inevitably, I suppose, I am more sceptical and cautious of the club's new owners, Fenway Sports Group, simply because of what went on under Hicks and Gillett. Once bitten, twice shy.

That is not particularly fair on John W. Henry, but it is not a bad thing either. Liverpool cannot be allowed to suffer again like it suffered under Hicks and Gillett. So far no one can say FSG have not made money available for signings and I know for a fact that they are trying their best to resolve the stadium issue, whether we should stay or move from Anfield, despite facing all sorts of complications.

Time will tell if they are good owners or not.

EL NINO

It seems strange to admit it now, but I had doubts about whether Fernando Torres would be a success at Liverpool.

Two things came into my head when he signed in the summer of 2007 for £20.5m from Atletico Madrid. I thought he could bomb because he would not be able to cope with the intensity and physicality of the Premier League having come from Spain and it would be another expensive mistake in the transfer market for the club. But I desperately hoped he would be the signing to take us to the next level. And what a signing he proved to be.

During his hot streak for Liverpool over the next few seasons, Torres was easily the best player I have ever played with in my career. I loved him.

I used to walk onto the pitch every single game convinced I was going to set up a goal for him or score myself. Sometimes I didn't. Mostly it seemed I did. I knew it was going to happen because Fernando was with me out there. At times, I felt invincible with him in the team alongside me.

In the first training sessions after he arrived, I recognised that his movement was very similar to that of Michael Owen. I thought to myself that I used to love playing with Michael and quickly came round to thinking my initial doubts had been stupid.

Torres was like Michael, but with more power. Sometimes if you played a difficult ball to Michael, the defenders were too big for him and they would win it back. Torres would make bad balls look good. That is how strong and powerful he was. He was a nightmare for defenders, but an absolute dream for me. I used to sit next to him in the dressing room because the pegs for our squad numbers – 8 and 9 – were next to each other and we'd talk like team-mates do.

I wouldn't say we were overly close. Torres is a really quiet person, although it would be wrong to call him a loner. He was comfortable with the Spanish lads we had in the team like Pepe, Xabi and Alvaro Arbeloa,

and the South Americans like Javier Mascherano, but we had a mutual respect of each other and we worked out pretty quickly that we needed one another to shine. He knew that if he made a good run, I would find him, but he also helped to make me become a more potent player as well.

I owe Rafa Benitez a great deal for my development as a player. When Rafa was appointed I had played right-back, and I had also played on the right of midfield from time to time, but I was essentially a box-to-box central midfielder. Rafa helped to make me a more disciplined midfielder and taught me how to time my runs better, which helped me get more goals.

When I went onto the right flank, although I didn't feel totally comfortable out there, he helped me become a good player there as well. I realised about the sacrifices you make for the team because at that point Liverpool were better setting up with two holding midfielders and, without sounding big-headed, I was enjoying a spell where not being in the middle did not unduly affect the level of my performances.

After that, Rafa helped me become a 'No.10' – someone who plays behind the striker – which I didn't think I even had in my armoury. I think the key to my success in that position was Torres. I always need to play with someone who can run in behind defences.

I played the odd game there with Dirk Kuyt and Peter Crouch, but that was different. I was the one who had to run in behind and I had to try and get their flick-ons. It wasn't the same. Torres would stretch defences, wreaking all manner of havoc, and that gave me space to exploit as well. Together we scored 111 goals in 117 games. Prolific.

The only downside was that we didn't win anything together. My boyhood club is Liverpool. Torres' boyhood club is Atletico Madrid. He left there in search of trophies and though we reached the semi-finals of competitions, we fell short.

It became obvious that he wasn't happy at Liverpool, but his departure in 2011 still hit me hard. Very hard. Every player is entitled to do what they want to do in their career. I don't own anyone else's career and I can't make decisions for them. But when you love

> **Torres would make bad balls look good. That is how strong he was.**

playing with someone and you have a player alongside you of Torres' calibre, then you cannot help but feel sorry for yourself and the fans who adored him. You wonder where the club is going if the best players want to leave, but I didn't feel let down by Liverpool.

There was nothing they could do to prevent him from leaving for Chelsea. His mind was set, but they made it as hard as they could for the £50m deal to happen.

In the days before the transfer, Torres came to see me as captain. He said he wanted to leave, but added that the club was being difficult. 'Listen,' I said. 'You have to understand that you are a top player and they don't want to let you go.' It didn't matter. He asked if I could speak to Kenny Dalglish, our manager, on his behalf. That put me in a difficult situation because I didn't want to help Fernando. I didn't want to tell the manager that the star player wanted to go because, at that point, I wanted the deal to fall through. I wanted Chelsea's interest to go away and for his enthusiasm to be rekindled. We had just signed Luis Suarez from Ajax for £22m. Money was available. We were trying to compete for silverware.

Fernando had told Kenny himself, but, with the club still playing hardball, he asked me to speak as well. I just told Kenny he was unhappy and left it at that. That is the role of the captain that people don't see and that I never want to experience again. You don't want your best player to come to you and say, 'I've had enough. I want to go to another club. And I want to go to one of your major rivals.'

When Fernando approached me and said he wanted out, it was like a knife to the heart.

Another Footballing Temple

I have scored seven career goals against Newcastle, a tally bettered only by my record against Aston Villa. St James' Park – it will always be known as that for me – is a great stadium. The fans are proper football supporters. If the club is going through a hard time, they still turn out in their droves. I'm glad they are in the Premier League and doing well.

Equalling Owen's Record

I don't really compare myself to the
likes of Michael Owen and Ian Rush
where goal records are concerned
because I have probably played
in more games than them, or scored
against weaker opposition.
Of course, it is flattering to hold
records at Liverpool. Here a penalty
against FC Porto allows me to match
Michael's tally of 22 European goals
for Liverpool. I would go on to set
a new record a few weeks later
when I scored against Marseille,
scrambling home a loose ball after
Steve Mandanda had saved my
initial penalty.

Stevie on the Spot

Keeping my nerve from the penalty spot became a feature of our run in the Champions League that season. We played Arsenal in the quarter-finals of the competition and after a 1-1 draw at The Emirates we fought out an enthralling battle at Anfield. When Emmanuel Adebayor made it 2-2 on the night, 3-3 on aggregate, with six minutes left we were staring at elimination. Ryan Babel earned a penalty straight away and it was up to me to dispatch the chance and reassert our authority. The pressure was on. All I could do was pick my spot and hope. Although Manuel Almunia went the right way, the penalty was too precise for him.

A Kiss for Good Luck

The Champions League in 2007-08 was nerve-shredding. We almost went out in the group stages, but clambered off the canvas, scoring 16 goals as we won our last three matches to qualify.

Then we played Inter Milan followed by Arsenal to set up another showdown with Chelsea. After beating them twice before in semi-finals, we were aiming to maintain our lucky streak.

Flying High, but Soon Grounded

We had conceded an advantage at Anfield when John Arne Riise scored a last-minute own goal to allow Chelsea to leave Merseyside with a 1-1 draw. It was a physical battle at Stamford Bridge, one that ebbed into extra time after Fernando Torres had cancelled out Didier Drogba's goal in normal time. But it wasn't to be our year. Chelsea prevailed before losing to Manchester United in the final in Moscow.

Collector's Item

You won't often see me taking a
throw-in for Liverpool. Not unless
we are in a rush, desperately trying
to get a goal, or I've been tackled
by the touchline and I can see a
team-mate in space. I am usually
stationed in the centre of the pitch
so a lot of the throw-ins are taken by
the full-backs. When Fabio Capello
was England manager, he would
hate players simply throwing the ball
down the line where a rival could
challenge for it. Capello wanted
throw-ins taken to a team-mate, and
for possession to be kept. It sounds
nit-picking, but it makes sense.

CHAPTER 12

2008
—
2009

CHANGING LANDSCAPE

It will be a miracle if I now realise my dream of winning the title with Liverpool and of hoisting the League Championship trophy towards the Kop. I know that sounds stark when it is written down and read out loud, but I am not soft. I'm not giving up, but I'm realistic and I am honest. Simple as that. Liverpool will rescale the heights one day, but, on a personal note, time is against me now.

One of the first pieces of advice my dad gave to me was that if you always do your best at something then no one will complain if, in the final reckoning, it ends up not being good enough. I would give my left arm for a title winners' medal, but if at the end of my career I have fallen short I know it will not have been through a lack of trying from me or my team-mates. We have been close and it is not too long ago that the core of the Liverpool team was as good as anyone in Europe.

I've spoken about the impact Fernando Torres had on my game, we had Carra at the back, and there was another person who contributed to the success of our partnership and that was Xabi Alonso.

He was a magician in midfield. The hub of everything we attempted. Every time Alonso's name comes up in conversation, people will instantly say: 'fantastic passer', and he is. I would have so much time on the ball because invariably Alonso would find me and do it so quickly that the opposition did not have time to react.

But despite the cleverness and speed of his passing, that was not the most obvious thing that struck me about him. Actually it was his work rate and his toughness. Xabi is a tough, tough boy.

So when you look at the spine of the team we had for a few seasons, you could not help but be impressed. Pepe Reina, probably the best goalkeeper in the world for a spell after he signed; Jamie Carragher, who between 2004 and 2010 was one of Europe's best defenders; there was Alonso, who has proved himself to be one of the best passers year after year after year; and alongside him was the Argentina captain, Javier Mascherano, clearing up all the mess and doing all the unheralded work.

I was enjoying my football and playing well, and in attack there was Torres at the very top of his game. One chance, one goal. I revelled playing alongside those players. It is open to debate, but in my mind that spine was better than the core group of players who won the Treble in 2000-01. It was just that the overall team wasn't as strong. If we had been a bit more astute in the transfer market around the time when Alonso was pulling the strings and Torres was scoring for fun, then that team would have won the league.

No doubt about it, we fell a bit short, but I don't think anyone has an argument with me that the core of that team didn't deserve, or wasn't good enough, to win the league. We finished second to Manchester United in

2009, three points off the top, but despite that small margin, it always felt as though it was a struggle to keep up. Rafa used to say to us all the time: 'Focus on the next game. Just the next game.' But when you haven't won the league before, you lack the experience to do that, and you start looking ahead and thinking, 'If we win this game and they don't win that and if that happens...'

You can't help but get carried away and dream. That is the difference between, say, Liverpool, and Manchester United and Chelsea. I hate to say it, but you can add Manchester City to that now, too. They have won the hardest title they will ever have to win because they now possess the know-how and the experience to do it all over again. You can't buy that – even with all the money they have at their disposal.

So it didn't happen for us again and when you are at the coal face, you cannot blame anyone but yourselves for not pulling it off. We are responsible for getting results and we fell short. There is no use in pointing fingers, but, at the same time, you cannot help but look back and think 'what if'. Liverpool provided funds initially and you can't ask a club to go out of its comfort zone in a financial sense just to make a player happy. The sad thing is seeing how that team

> **"He was a magician in midfield. The hub of everything we attempted."**

has fragmented, although to be honest you have to expect it with foreign players and you can't afford to be too emotional towards them when they do move on. Look at Mascherano. He had the chance to go to Barcelona and I don't know any South American in the world who doesn't want to play at the Nou Camp.

Xabi Alonso had his own problems, which began when Rafa wanted to bring Gareth Barry in and move Xabi on in the summer of 2008. I don't blame Xabi for then getting his agent to see what was out there. It is hard for a Spaniard to turn Real Madrid down, especially when the manager had tried to sell Xabi when he was settled at the club. When some players move they go on about how they are huge Liverpool fans and why leaving is 'killing' them. Xabi was genuinely gutted to go. He loved the club and believe me when I say he is a true Liverpool fan. Before every big game he has I will text him and wish him good luck. He does the same to me. A great player, but a great lad, too.

So the owners have tried, managers and players have tried, but we have so far fallen short. We have to accept that. I will never give up on that dream of winning the title. It's just going to be tough because I know I am running out of time.

Biding My Time

I hate being a substitute for many reasons. For one it suggests that I may be easing my way back after an injury, or that the manager has decided to rest me from his starting line-up. Then there is the fact that when you are warming up on the touchline, the stick you get from some of the crowds in England can be relentless. The best atmosphere, other than Anfield, I have ever played in came against Besiktas in Istanbul in 2007. We lost the game 2-1, but the atmosphere their fans generated was unbelievable. They stood up and were bouncing for 90 minutes. That was a hostile environment.

Gratitude

I'm either pointing towards one of my team-mates by way of thanking him for setting me up with another goal, or I am picking out one of my family members in the crowd. My dad and brother come and watch me all the time. It's good for me to share my success with them. They have made sacrifices in their lives to help me reach the top.

Keep Calm

The most dangerous part of any game is when you have just scored. Everyone is on a high and concentration can lapse in moments like that. Fernando had just scored against Everton in a Merseyside derby at Goodison Park and I am trying to tell the team that we've still got work to do, that we cannot get carried away. That is the role of a captain sometimes. It worked anyway because Fernando scored again and we won 2-0.

Set-piece Specialist

You can see from the shape of my body that I am trying to whip this set-piece right into the centre of the penalty area. Putting pace on corners can cause problems for defenders and open the door for attackers. This corner came at Fulham, a team with players such as Brede Hangeland, Bobby Zamora and Dickson Etuhu – all tall players. They would've had a better chance of relieving the pressure if I had just floated the ball across with little pace.

Jump for Joy

We played Everton three times
in the space of a fortnight at the
start of 2009: once in the league
and twice in the FA Cup. We didn't
win any of the matches, drawing
twice at Anfield and losing a replay
at Goodison Park in which I had
hobbled off with a torn hamstring.
I scored in both the Anfield games
and I always milk my celebrations
against Everton because of the
amount of stick I get from their fans.
But I would rather have won
the games.

Move Over Madrid

If you look at the players in the Real Madrid team we met in the Champions League this season, it shows what a brilliant performance we produced. Heinze, Robben, Cannavaro, Casillas, Ramos, Raul, Sneijder – and yet they couldn't live with us. We won 1-0 in the Bernabeu thanks to a header from Yossi Benayoun, a great player and friend, and then battered them at Anfield 4-0. I scored twice.

Kiss Me Quick

There are just some days when everything goes right for the team. We were confident going to Old Trafford because we had just beaten Real Madrid 4-0 in the Champions League, but no one expected us to beat Manchester United 4-1 on their own patch. This was when Fernando was at his peak, scaring the life out of defenders such as Nemanja Vidic and Rio Ferdinand. He equalised and I dispatched another penalty before noticing the Sky cameras nearby and running over and planting a kiss on the screen. The celebration was to wind up the United fans, but also for my daughters watching at home.

Good Things Come in Threes

We produced a spell of football around the March of that season that was as good as anything I can remember in my time. We were swatting teams aside. Good teams as well. Aston Villa came to Anfield and we were on fire. I scored a hat-trick that day, including two more penalties, and finished the season with 24 goals.

Last-minute Winner

There is no better feeling than
scoring a last-minute winner. We had
been trailing at home against
Middlesbrough until the 86th minute
when they scored an own goal and
I managed to find the back of the
net in injury time to seal a 2-1
success. Anfield erupts at moments
such as that and the dressing room
afterwards is buzzing. Belief is
important in any football team and
it is games like this, which tilt in your
favour right at the death, that allow
you to dream and think anything is
possible. It proves you should never
give up or sulk about things when
they are not going your way. There
is always time to alter history. It just
depends how you use that time.

One Captain to Another

Having inherited the captain's armband from Sami Hyypia, it was my pleasure to hand it back to him as he said farewell to Liverpool after 10 years of brilliant service. Sami had announced he was leaving the club to move to Germany and this was his chance to say goodbye to the fans. He came on with six minutes left, which I thought was very harsh of Rafa. I kept looking to the sidelines in the game, thinking: 'When is Sami coming on?' We had nothing to play for against Tottenham apart from pride and I think that he should have started the game.

The Full Set

Having previously won the PFA Young Player of the Year and Players' Player of the Year awards, it was nice to complete the hat-trick by being voted the Football Writers' Association Footballer of the Year in 2009. I am hugely appreciative of the honour, especially when you consider the standard of players in England.

CHAPTER 13

2009
—
2010

THE MANAGERIAL MERRY-GO-ROUND

Rafa Benitez is the best coach I have played for.
Tactically he is very astute, he undoubtedly made me a better player and I respect him. But I understand why he was sacked by Liverpool in the summer of 2010. Everything felt a mess at that point and it was the right time for a change. Rafa had become embroiled in fights with different people at the club and lost his focus on what his strengths were. His job was to coach the team, it wasn't to get into political battles and it seemed best for everyone – the club, the players and also Rafa – that there was a break and the slate wiped clean.

We had disappointed that season, finishing seventh in the Premier League and crashing out of the Champions League. It looked like our season could still end with a silver lining as we progressed through the Europa League, but we fluffed the semi-final against Atletico Madrid and ended up watching them lift the trophy.

Rafa could have continued into the new season, but the first sign of a set-back and the atmosphere would have turned poisonous again. That would have been no good to anyone. Again there were whispers that it was the players who said: 'Push the button. Get rid of him.' But that just makes me frustrated and angry. It was Liverpool's board of directors who made a decision they believed to be in the best interests of the club. All the rumours suggesting otherwise simply harm reputations and harm relationships with managers.

OK, so I don't think I will be going out for a meal with Rafa any time soon, but if he had been in charge on the first day of the following season I would have stood

in the dressing room before the kick-off and told my team-mates this was the campaign in which we would achieve something. And from the moment the first whistle went, I would have been giving 100% because it is Liverpool Football Club.

I feared for Roy Hodgson almost as soon as he became Liverpool's new manager. I feared for him because he was not Kenny Dalglish. I have no doubt that if Roy had arrived at Anfield at a different time in the club's history, he would have done well. The demands and expectations, the history and tradition at Liverpool make it one of the most difficult jobs in football, but I believe he could have made a success of things with the right support.

But from the moment the club overlooked Kenny as a replacement for Rafa, it was always going to be difficult for Roy. Kenny is the number one hero of everyone at Liverpool: the fans, the staff, the players. He was itching to step back into management, desperate for the chance to return to the club he loves and where he had been so successful previously. I totally understand why there was such a groundswell of opinion among supporters for Kenny and that made things tough for Roy.

Tough, but not impossible. There is a lot said about the way teams play under Roy. Negative is a harsh criticism of him. Cautious? Maybe that's fair. But then Gerard Houllier and Rafa were cautious as well at times.

When you are playing against the best teams at the top level, if you are not sensible, if you are not disciplined and if you are not cautious, then you are going to get beaten. It's common sense. But I wouldn't say England were cautious when we were losing 2-1 against Sweden at Euro 2012 and Roy sent on Theo Walcott to help the team win 3-2. His style could have worked.

Managers become good managers with good players and the right personnel around them. Don't forget that at that time, Javier Mascherano left Liverpool and once again not all the money was being reinvested into the team. Roy was also on the trail of Luis Suarez at that point but we couldn't afford him, and some of his other signings, like Paul Konchesky and Christian Poulsen, didn't work out.

Still, there is no point making excuses. Roy also knows football is about results and we didn't win enough matches.

You could smell pretty quickly that it wasn't going to work out. We lost to Northampton in the Carling Cup and Blackpool at home in the Premier League and were soon on a downward trajectory. The atmosphere was deteriorating.

I remember after we lost 1-0 to Wolves in December, a defeat that ended with boos ringing around Anfield again, going to my car and a fan shouting over towards me. 'Hey Gerrard, you're the captain, get it sorted. You want to have a look at yourself,' he said (and that's minus the swear words) as he peered through the huge iron gates by the Centenary Stand.

> **You could smell pretty quickly that it wasn't going to work out.**

My initial reaction was to go over to him and front it up face-to-face, but I ignored him. It wouldn't have looked good if I'd started rowing with a fan. Someone with a camera phone takes a picture of us and the next thing I am on the front of a national newspaper, adding to the problems. We had enough of those without me making it worse. I did the right thing.

Liverpool fans are the best in the world. That is not just me being biased. There have been hundreds of football people who have no ties with the club, but have visited Anfield and said the same. Fact. But like with everything, there are a handful who are daft. It's like the supporter who took £20 to burn one of my shirts outside Melwood in front of the Sky Sports cameras around the time of all the stuff about me going to Chelsea. I understand the frustration, but from the first time I pulled on a Liverpool shirt I have been doing everything I can to 'get it sorted'.

If the fan who shouted at me after the Wolves game sits back and thinks about my contribution over the years, then hopefully he will recognise that he was wrong.

Roy was sacked not long after that debacle, the shortest reign of any Liverpool manager, but he is a good man and an honest man, and my respect for him is not diminished by his time at the club.

The 500 Club

When I walked off the pitch on my debut against Blackburn, it was with a real sense of accomplishment. Never mind I had only been on a few minutes, I'd played for Liverpool. It was a dream I never thought I would realise. Then you get greedy. You want to play again and again and again.

To pull on a Liverpool shirt 500 times is something I am hugely proud of. It was nice of the club to commemorate the milestone with Rafa and managing director Christian Purslow presenting me with an award as I hold Lilly-Ella and Lexie. The next target is 600, which isn't too far away.

Rallying the Troops

I would always prefer to lead
through my actions rather than
words, but sometimes the occasion
demands it. I try not to rant and rave
as a captain, but look to choose
my moments to speak. Otherwise,
people can switch off if they are
hearing the same voice over and
over again. There have been a lot
of changes at Liverpool in recent
years, new players coming in and
young, foreign players arriving – that
is when I have to step up as skipper.
It is important to make people feel
welcome off the pitch and make
sure that on it they understand what
playing for Liverpool is all about.

Blood, Sweat and No Tears

Beating Everton always pleases me because I know how badly our fans feel when they turn up for work on a Monday morning and have to take a load of stick from their Evertonian mates. David Moyes has done a really good job at Goodison Park and helped Everton finish above Liverpool on a couple of occasions in the Premier League. That hurts, but we still have a good record in head-to-heads against them and that means a lot. Arms aloft, teeth gritted, you can see what winning against our neighbours means to me.

I'm No Dummy

You can imagine the stick I took when I walked into the dressing room the day after this shot appeared in the papers. I'd kept it quiet that I had been approached by Madame Tussauds because I knew what would follow. Carra and Pepe Reina were the ring leaders, passing comment on my hairstyle and my nose among the cleaner stuff I can reveal. I was hugely flattered, if a little embarrassed, when they said they wanted to produce a waxwork dummy of me. I think the likeness is really good. The real Steven Gerrard is the one on the left just in case you can't tell.

These Boots Were Made For Talking

As soon as I signed a boot deal with adidas as a teenager, they put 'Gerrard' on my boots. It was a bit embarrassing at first because I'd only played a handful of games and some of the senior players at the club might've thought I was a 'Big Time Charlie'. Nowadays, of course, it's odd if you don't have your name on your boots.

It's a nice touch. This is the perfect boot for me because it's black. I can't be doing with those boots that are yellow, pink or orange. Maybe I'm boring, but give me a standard black boot any day. But I am on my own on that one it seems. Recently adidas were saying to me that black boots don't really sell well these days.

Always a Poignant Day

When my cousin, Jon-Paul Gilhooley, was nine he went to Hillsborough with his family to watch the FA Cup semi-final between Liverpool and Nottingham Forest. He did not come back. Jon-Paul was the youngest fan to lose his life that day. It is important for the club to never forget what happened at Hillsborough and never to forget the 96 fans who lost their lives supporting the club they love. Each year on the anniversary of the disaster, Liverpool hold a memorial service at Anfield. The players and staff attend and pay their respects to the dead and their families. It is personal for me because of Jon-Paul, and I will never forget. For the families of the Hillsborough victims, the battle for justice continues. Hopefully their persistence and dedication is going to pay off soon and the truth about what happened that day will finally come out in public. I admire their fight and resolve. I am with them.

CHAPTER 14

2010
—
2011

KING KENNY RETURNS

In the games' room at my house, I have the shirts of some of the players I have been lucky enough to play against, and also alongside, hanging on the wall.

Zidane, Ronaldinho, Xavi, Iniesta, Ronaldo, Totti, Keane, Vieira and Henry are all there, together with Torres, Alonso, Reina and Carragher. Thinking about it now, Carra has done well to get himself into such esteemed company!

But there was one shirt I wanted to make the room complete: Kenny Dalglish's. I knew Kenny before he came back as manager and so I tried my luck. He said he might have an old one in a box upstairs at his house somewhere and true enough he found it for me and signed the Number 7 shirt with a private message on it.

As much as I was disappointed that things didn't work out for Roy Hodgson – because I think he is a top coach – at Liverpool Football Club, when results are not good, inevitably changes will happen no matter who is in charge. Things couldn't carry on like they were. We were in the middle of the table and not certain of climbing it, which is ridiculous when you consider the quality of the players we still had.

Liverpool supporters have a powerful voice and when they speak, you have to listen. It was clear who they wanted to take over, they had been singing Kenny's name as early into the season as October, and I knew Kenny walking through the door in January 2011 would give everyone a lift.

In an instant, the club was united again. Everyone was on the same page, no one was fighting and the club's new owners made money available for transfers. Torres left, but Luis Suarez and Andy Carroll arrived as we broke the club's record transfer fee twice in a matter of hours.

When Andy came he took time to settle and find his form. Playing for Newcastle is different to playing for Liverpool. The pressure is different and that is not me being disrespectful. I think he understands that now and in the second half of the season he was on fire and a handful for the opposition. He has the potential to be one of the best strikers around.

Suarez, on the other hand, made the transition into English football seamlessly. I love training and playing with him. He is a magician, a player who can conjure something out of nothing and I just hope that Liverpool can satisfy his ambitions and that he stays at the club for years to come. There are not many players like Luis in the world, someone who lights up the pitch as soon as he steps onto it and I just wish I'd played alongside more often up to now.

The delight I took at seeing Kenny back at Liverpool was tempered on a personal level by the fact that I didn't feature for him as much as I would have liked. I was sent off in his first game, an FA Cup tie versus Manchester United, and then injuries took hold. Of the 16 months that Kenny spent back in charge, I probably missed 10 months of that time. That is a major regret, but there was nothing I could do because of both my injuries.

Before I broke down with a ruptured groin in the March, Kenny knows what I went through for him, the club and for my team-mates just to get out onto the pitch. I was like a pin cushion, taking injections in order to play.

At the time you don't worry about the effects because you have a game against Manchester United in three days and you need to win. The fans want you out there.

There are two groups of players in football. There are those who will do anything to get out on the pitch and there are players who won't. When you have an injection, you are basically trying to cover the problem up. I knew I wasn't doing my body any good, and that my groin was becoming weaker. I knew the risks.

We were training at Melwood one Friday before a game at West Brom and I twisted. Bang. My groin ruptured. One sharp movement and it came completely off the bone. Agony, complete and utter agony. I was out for six months, my comeback delayed by an infection, but in the back of my mind I at least knew that the surgery had been a success. Liverpool had done medical tests that showed my groin was stronger than it had been for the best part of a decade.

My comeback lasted five games. There have been so many rumours about why I picked up a second infection, but the truth is it was a freak accident. I had gone up for a header with Daniel Agger in training and when he landed, he caught me on my ankle. It was the sort of graze caused by a stud mark that I have suffered a million times before, the sort of knock I wouldn't even show anyone.

But overnight my ankle started swelling and growing like never before. Even then I travelled down to West Brom with the team and was going to have another injection to play, although I seriously wondered whether I would even be able to get my boot on because the joint had ballooned up so much.

> **I was like a pin cushion, taking injections in order to play.**

Liverpool's doctor, Zaf Iqbal, did a blood test and sent it away to a laboratory for tests. I was just sitting down for an evening meal at the team hotel when he said I needed to go back to Liverpool immediately. My first thought was that something had happened to my family, but then Zaf told me about the infection and said it needed to be treated straight away.

In those situations, you have to put your trust in the medical people and I am lucky in that I have total faith in Zaf and I also have one of the best physios around in Chris Morgan.

Two hours after sitting down for pasta, I was in the Spire Hospital in Liverpool having an operation to drain my ankle and clear up the infection. My career was saved on that operating table not only by the skill of the surgeon, Chris Walker, but also the speed of thought of Zaf and Chris Morgan.

Roy Imparts the Wisdom of Experience

I will always maintain that Roy Hodgson could have proved he was the right man for Liverpool. His reign was short-lived because he was appointed at the wrong time. Liverpool supporters are powerful and when they call for something it is hard to resist. Roy came in to replace Rafa in the summer of 2010, but I feared he was up against it from the start because the fans wanted their idol, Kenny Dalglish, to take over. When the team didn't then hit the ground running, it was always going to be tough for Roy. I respect him and I like him and I think with the right players he could have been a success at Anfield. He was very good to me and Jamie Carragher. He loved Jamie as a player and I just wish, as a group, we could have got better results.

Leading From the Front

I'm often perceived to be the leader in the Liverpool team, but it simply isn't like that. I am the captain and I do my share of organising and, hopefully, leading by example, but I am not on my own. Carra is a leader in his own right and I believe Pepe Reina is a future Liverpool skipper. Pepe's a very strong character, which is a bit of a prerequisite for a goalkeeper because it can be a lonely position at times. But he is also unselfish, genuine and most of all he commands the respects of his team-mates.

Enjoying the Moment

It's not just my reaction that shows how good it is to score against Manchester United, but my team- mates' as well. We were losing 2-0 in this game at Old Trafford before getting it back to 2-2. My first goal came from a free-kick and had a little good fortune about it as it crept through a gap in United's defensive wall. Unfortunately, my joy was short-lived. Dimitar Berbatov started that season on fire and his hat-trick against us that day was one of the reasons why.

A Liverpool Legend and a True Friend

England had played Bulgaria in a European Championship qualifier at Wembley the night before and we had another game with Switzerland looming, but nothing was going to stop me from playing in Jamie Carragher's Testimonial match. I desperately wanted to show my appreciation to a team-mate and friend, whose achievement in playing for Liverpool for so long should not be overlooked. It is difficult to play for Liverpool's first team week in, week out for the best part of 15 years as Carra has done. More so because he is a local lad, too. He is rightly considered to be a legend.

Conversing with King Kenny

As much as I was disappointed that Roy Hodgson's tenure was over almost before it had begun, I knew for the sake of the club that a change was needed. Kenny was itching to get back and when he answered the owners' call to return to the Liverpool dug-out for the first time in 20 years his impact was like flicking a switch. Straight away the club was unified. The supporters were behind their hero, the players benefited from his man-management and Liverpool felt like Liverpool again. What I like about Kenny is that he will defend the club to the day he dies. He loves Liverpool, it is his life. I'd be sitting at home some days and his weekly press conference would be on Sky Sports News and he'd say something like, 'Yes, they've got good players but we've not got bad ones ourselves.' He was only interested in Liverpool doing well, and the way we finished that season showed how he was successful in stripping away all the negativity that had been plaguing us before.

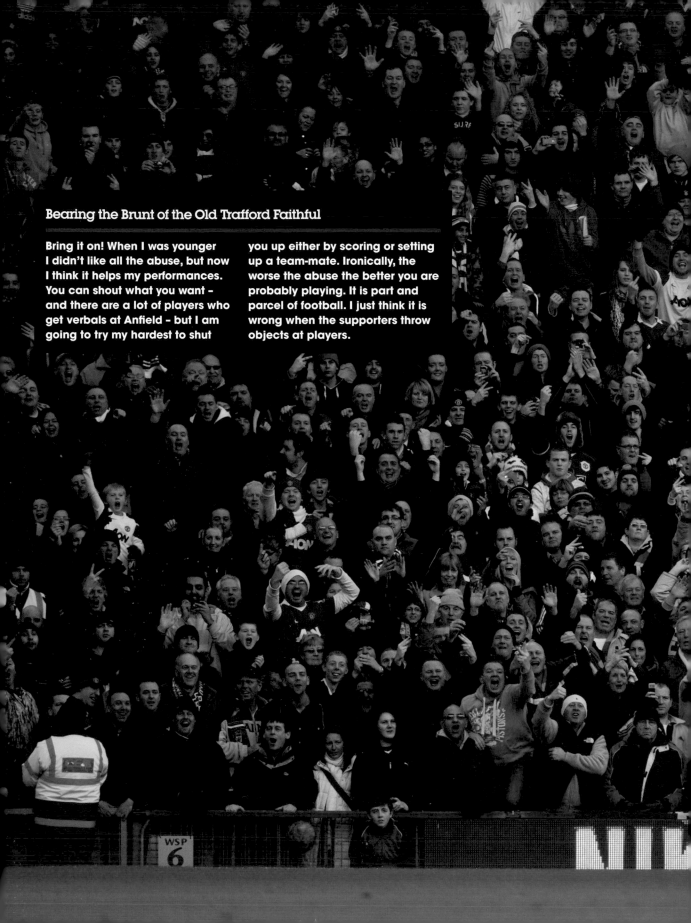

Bearing the Brunt of the Old Trafford Faithful

Bring it on! When I was younger I didn't like all the abuse, but now I think it helps my performances. You can shout what you want – and there are a lot of players who get verbals at Anfield – but I am going to try my hardest to shut you up either by scoring or setting up a team-mate. Ironically, the worse the abuse the better you are probably playing. It is part and parcel of football. I just think it is wrong when the supporters throw objects at players.

Face to Face With Fernando Again

This was the day I hoped I would never see. Fernando was such a massive player for Liverpool and a massive influence on my own game that seeing him leave was hard. Watching him go to Chelsea was even harder. In some respects, he will argue that the move he made has been justified. He was part of Chelsea's Champions League and FA Cup winning squads, but I know it will hurt him not to have started either game. There were days during his time at Anfield when he was unplayable, when I knew he would score even before the game had kicked off. I hope he gets back to that standard, except, of course, for the games when I am staring across the pitch at him.

Free Wheelers

The facilities at Melwood are first class and they cater for a player's every need there. Gerard Houllier deserves a lot of credit for this because he recognised the necessity to create a new state-of-the-art facility on the complex. The old Melwood was a few dressing rooms, a small gym and a canteen. Before training sometimes, we will go on the exercise bikes just to warm up our muscles and it's good to get everyone together. There are a lot more British players at the club now and that can help team spirit, although ultimately it is down to how good you are not where you come from. Carra's leading the banter here as Andy Carroll, Joe Cole and I look on. No change there then.

A Face in the Crowd

I was injured for the end of the 2010-11 season, but decided to attend the final game of the campaign away at Aston Villa. Basically, I was a fan for a day. Carra had done it a few years ago and I'd had a few letters saying I should go to an away game. It was an eye-opener for me to get in among the supporters. I think for a young player in our squad, or maybe one of the foreign lads, to have a day like that would really help them.

Why not? The fans absolutely adore the players. The players get so much support from the fans, so I think for a player to give up a day, mix with the fans and give a little back ...well, there's no harm in that. Yes, there was a bit of banter flying around. Stuff like, 'You won't get back in the team, Stevie,' and 'You've got a fight on next season, Gerrard, to get past Lucas and Spearo (Jay Spearing).' I think it was all good natured!

CHAPTER 15

2011 — 2012

A BRACE OF CUP FINALS... BUT KING KENNY DEPARTS

My mobile phone rang and Kenny's name came up on the screen. I was half expecting what he was going to say, but it remains one of the saddest conversations I've had. After leading Liverpool to two Cup Finals, winning the Carling Cup, I genuinely thought that Kenny would be in charge for the start of the new season. When Kenny went with Steve Clarke, his assistant, to Boston to see the club's owners after the final game of the season, I thought it would be to discuss the plans for the new campaign and transfer budgets. But when he flew home without any assurances, I feared what was coming.

I think Kenny deserved more time, but football is a cut-throat business. Kenny, more than anyone, knows that eighth place is not good enough for Liverpool Football Club, but that league position was false.

I don't look for excuses. Every club can say 'what if' about their season. What if Manchester United hadn't conceded a late goal at home to Everton in that 4-4 draw? They would be champions. You have to deal with the set-backs you endure. Having said that, if you watched Liverpool from the start through to the finish of last season, there was no way that we were the eighth best team in the Premier League. We were far better than that and didn't deserve to finish there. I genuinely feel that if we went into the final couple of games with a chance of still qualifying for the Champions League that would have been more representative of how we played. I think we hit the woodwork 33 times – we couldn't do that again if we tried – and missed numerous other gilt-edged chances, drawing too many games at Anfield in the process. I still believe in this team and we are due the rub of the green.

Also, the fact we reached two Cup Finals shows there are good players at this club. You don't beat Chelsea and Manchester City en route to lifting the Carling Cup if your team is rubbish. And when you come within a yard, less than that, of keeping your hopes alive in the FA Cup Final as well, then that shows your team-mates don't lack heart and character.

The Carling Cup often gets dismissed as meaningless, but you cannot underestimate its importance to Liverpool last season.

Reaching the final allowed us to dream again and winning the trophy ended a six-year barren spell without silverware for the club. That is too long for Liverpool FC.

Meeting Cardiff City at Wembley was a landmark day for the Gerrards, but one that would ultimately end in both joy and despair. My cousin, Anthony, has forged a great career for himself since finding it difficult to make progress at Everton, and he can be proud of what he has done. He's younger than me, but I am quite close to him. I can remember, growing up, we'd play together at Ironside Road where my grandparents lived.

As always with Liverpool, we made life difficult for ourselves during the game. I think the occasion got to some of our players and we also found ourselves trying too hard, myself included.

What I thought would be a comfortable success, and I mean no disrespect to Cardiff by that, turned into a slog. We fell behind, hauled ourselves level through Martin Skrtel, took the lead thanks to Dirk Kuyt, and then conceded at the death, which lead to extra time and then penalties.

I should have known what was coming. Birmingham in 2001, AC Milan 2005, West Ham 2006, if we can find the hard way to do something, we will. The shoot-out did not start well. I was first up and saw my attempt well saved by Tom Heaton, the Cardiff goalkeeper. The walk back to the half-way line was tortuous. Every step of the way, I was thinking: 'I've just lost us the Cup.'

I wasn't on my own. Charlie Adam's effort went high and wide, while for Cardiff, Kenny Miller and Rudy Gestede were also off target. That meant that when Anthony stepped forward to take his kick, he had to succeed.

Instinctively, I celebrated when he dragged his shot just wide of Pepe Reina's post. It was an important moment for Liverpool, but I was heartbroken for Anthony. At times like that whatever you say seems hollow. I sought him out as the party began around him and looked to console him, but words are useless in those situations. Instead, I waited until the next day to speak to him properly. I know what he was going through. When you score an own goal in the last minutes of a Cup Final against a big team and one of your biggest rivals, there is no place to hide.

The other disappointment of that day for me was that the success did not become the platform that it should have been for the rest of the season. I still believe it was an important milestone in the development of this team, but we wasted the opportunity to prove that immediately.

> **I think Kenny deserved more time, but football is a cut-throat business.**

Our league form remained frustratingly inconsistent and, while the FA Cup left me dreaming of a Cup double, especially when we beat Everton in the semi-final at Wembley, that was to end in failure.

It still nags away at me as to why, as a team, we didn't turn up for the first hour of the final against Chelsea. There is no explanation for it. We knew what was at stake. It was inconceivable that we should be so insipid.

When we eventually woke up, of course, we pushed Chelsea close and the debate about whether Andy Carroll's header crossed the line or not raged afterwards. If we had come back to 2-2 and forced extra time, I am sure we would have won. Roberto di Matteo's side were out on their feet at that point.

Yet the manner of our comeback left me only with regrets. If only we had started like we had finished. If only: those two small words are the worst for any footballer.

Reaching two Finals and winning one trophy did not mask our league position, but it wasn't the worst season either. Liverpool is about winning silverware. It was important to return to that standard. What the decision to dismiss Kenny shows is that the Americans are not afraid of making big calls, good or bad. It shows they care about Liverpool. Now we have to see if it works.

Slide Rule

This was my first start back after my groin operation and the infection that slowed my rehabilitation. I'd made a few cameos before that, easing my way back in, but I have to thank Kenny for having the faith to pitch me in against Manchester United. It went better than I expected in the main and I scored a free-kick in front of the Kop before United equalised. The celebration was to show once and for all there were no ill-effects on my groin after the surgery. Being honest, the doctors probably winced when they saw me doing that.

Behold the Joy on Kenny's Face

It is sad the way Kenny's reign ended at the end of last season, but it hasn't changed how I look at him or what I feel for him. I don't think his departure will change the way too many Liverpool fans regard him either. Whether he is the manager or not, he is still an icon; someone who has given his life for Liverpool. The look on his face sums up perfectly his love for the club. Every time we scored a goal, you saw his celebration: arms in the air, beaming smile. People who have that kind of passion are very hard to find.

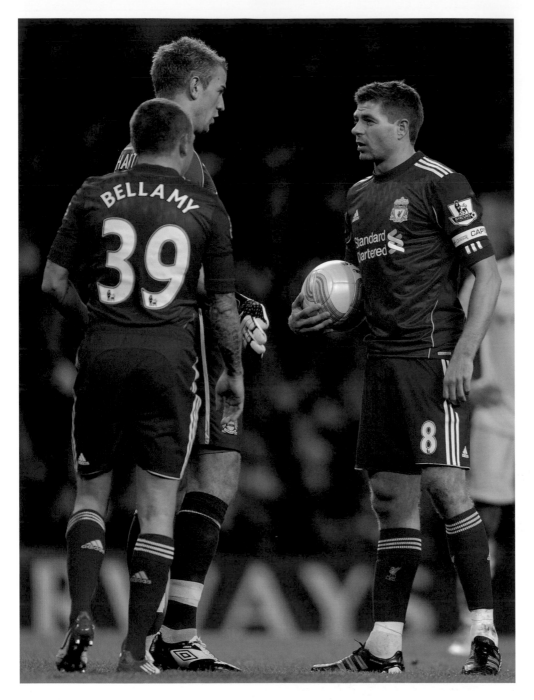

Joe Hart Tries to Psyche Me Out...

The semi-final of the Carling Cup last season pitted us against Manchester City and twice I found myself up against Joe Hart from the spot. You know the banter is coming. Joe's saying: 'I know where you are going to put it, you're going to miss this, the pressure is too big for you.' I'm just trying to stay focused and not get taken in by it all. I'm a little bit too long in the tooth to fall for those tactics.

... It Doesn't Work

As I have said, these days I pick my spot and stick to it. If the goalkeeper makes a save I will accept it and step forward the next time Liverpool get a penalty rather than rushing to the back of the queue. Twice in the space of a week, I found the back of the net against Joe and that was the best way to keep him quiet.

You could see during England's Euro 2012 shoot-out with Italy in the quarter-final that he was trying to psyche the Italians out of it as well. Make no mistake, Joe will be the best goalkeeper in the world one day. And when I say one day, I mean one day soon. He has a great presence and is a great lad.

Signing on the Dotted Line

Liverpool have said to me that when I finally hang up my boots, which hopefully won't be any time soon, there is an ambassadorial role waiting for me. I'm flattered and time will tell whether I go on to take up the offer. It is an option in the new contract I signed last season. I wanted two more years on top of the year I had left to run. The club offered me another 12 months, which I understand, given my age.

I could have kicked up a fuss, been hard work in the negotiations and chosen to go into the final year of my contract, but I am not that type of player. Here I'm putting pen to paper next to Damien Comolli, who was Director of Football. I signed a year extension, so my contract now runs out in the summer of 2014. Hopefully, I can prove between now and then that I am worth another one.

A Matter of Life and Death?

Like everyone in football, I was shocked to see what happened to Fabrice Muamba. He has always been a good opponent and I can remember on occasions when we played Bolton, he would man-mark me and make it a tough afternoon. I sent him a signed shirt during his recovery and I'm glad he is making such huge strides on his road to rehabilitation. What happened to him puts everything into perspective.

Close But No Cigar

Leading Liverpool back into a major final after so many years watching everyone else doing it was important for me. The Carling Cup often gets derided, but for Liverpool last season it was a massive competition, especially as we weren't playing in Europe. Once again we made life difficult for ourselves and, collectively, I felt we tried too hard at times, although Cardiff deserve credit for the way they played. I fared no better and snatched at this shot before seeing it sail over the crossbar. There is something in Liverpool's DNA that dictates that when we are cornered we come back fighting and usually get over the line.

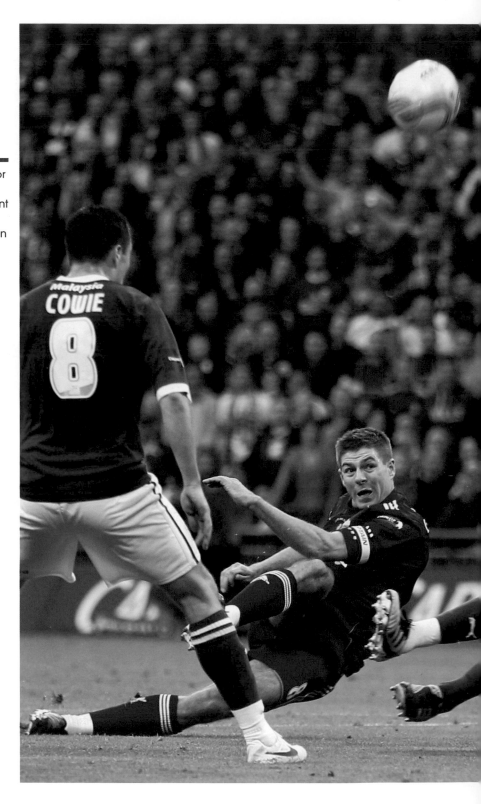

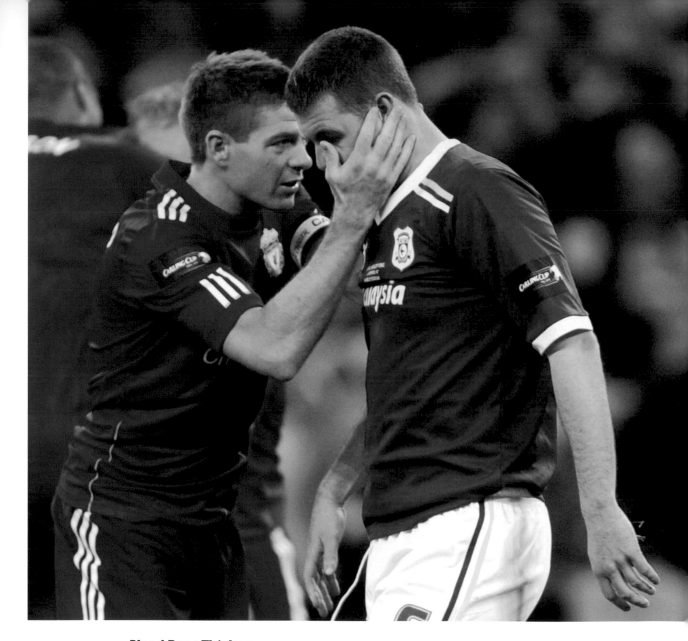

Blood Runs Thicker

Facing my cousin, Anthony Gerrard, in the final was a great day for my family. I knew it would mean joy for one of us and despair for the other. I missed my penalty in the shoot-out, just like Anthony missed his. Unfortunately for him, his miss was decisive. Football is governed by small details and that day proved it. I was devastated for him because I know how hard he has worked to forge a career for himself.

I said a few words at the time – 'Just keep your head up' – but called him the next day to chat in more detail. I scored an own goal in a League Cup Final and watched the trophy slip through our fingers as a result, before channelling my emotions and using the experience to motivate myself. Anthony will do the same. He's someone who meets challenges head on.

Another Trophy in the Cabinet

As I lifted the Carling Cup aloft, I felt it could be a springboard for the club. I haven't changed my view even though the rest of the season didn't pan out as we had expected. For many of the players at the club this was the first time they had tasted winning any silverware. It gives you the belief that you can go on and win more trophies and we came close to doing just that in the FA Cup Final against Chelsea a couple of months later. I'm certain that whole experience will stand us in good stead for the future.

1, 2, 3, Against Everton

Going into another Merseyside derby, we were under pressure. Our form hadn't been good. Everyone was telling us Everton were going to win at Anfield for the first time since I was sent off in 1999. David Moyes

rested players ahead of an FA Cup tie, but I still think we would have won had he picked a full strength team. It proved a good night for me personally. I grabbed a hat-trick and to do that against Everton rates

highly in my career. This was the final goal, although to be honest I barely had to do anything. Luis Suarez set me up brilliantly in front of the Kop. Hopefully, my partnership with Luis will fire this season, too.

The Greatest Feeling in the World

I always relish scoring against Everton and I have clear memories of the goals I have managed against them throughout my career. I think this picture shows just what the battle for bragging rights means to me. Beating Everton doesn't make Liverpool's season, but for a few days afterwards you have a spring in your step. It is in matches against Everton and Manchester United that, as a player, I feel the responsibility we have in living out the fans' dreams even more.

Reverting to Childhood

I get abused mercilessly by Evertonians. They can criticise me all they want and there were times in the past when I enjoyed the banter. I took it as a sign that, deep down, they respect me as a player. Why bother shouting abuse at someone who you don't think is capable of hurting you on the pitch? But the abuse I get these days is about my family, which I don't like. I am never going to stop them singing their songs, but what I can do is to try and make sure they are not singing about a win for their team.

A Hat-trick Bun in the Oven

As with the 'sucking thumb' celebration, the match ball up my shirt gesture was one back at the Everton fans who target my family in their songs. I had been given the ball for scoring a hat-trick against them. It was just my way of saying, 'All go home and sing your songs, but remember who scored the hat-trick.' I've done quite well against Everton over the years, but the treble I got last season was hugely satisfying. As good as it was, it's gone now. If you linger on your achievements in football, you'll go backwards. I know I won't score a hat-trick against Everton every time I face them, but the odd goal wouldn't go amiss.

Another One Slips Away

The two finals we reached last season were so important to me personally because at this stage of my career I don't know when I am going to experience that again. The FA Cup Final against Chelsea was an opportunity missed to collect my third winners' medal.

I probably have two or three chances left now to try and get that hat-trick. For an hour, we didn't play and Chelsea could have been out of sight. At the final whistle, we felt devastated because for the last 30 minutes we swarmed all over them. How many times have you heard that football is settled by the smallest of details? Well whether a ball – from Andy Carroll's header, in this case – has fully crossed the line or not is the perfect example of that. If it had gone to extra time we would have won. It didn't and I was left with regrets.

EPILOGUE

Whatever I achieve in my career from here on in is a bonus. After the last two injuries I have had, I am intent on enjoying every single minute I have left in the game.

I have spent too much time on the sidelines and when you are out of the team you realise just how lucky you are to be a footballer. That is why I am determined to make the most of the opportunities that I am sure will continue to come my way. My ambition hasn't altered and my will to win won't become diluted. I want to see Liverpool winning silverware. I want to see Liverpool challenging for the top four and getting back into the Champions League where this club belongs. And, more than anything, I want Liverpool to win the Premier League title. I will continue to give everything I can to try and ensure that happens. It will be hard, but I'm not scared of a challenge.

I think that outlook has served me well so far in my career and there is no reason to change now. But maybe, because of what I have been through in recent seasons, I won't get as down as I have in the past when things haven't gone according to plan. I say that now after I have returned from my summer holiday following Euro 2012, but I know it will be hard to stick to that and simply take any set-backs on the chin and move on when the new season starts.

Liverpool has undergone a lot of change (too much change in many respects, if you want to compete at the highest level), but I know that at the same time some of the changes in recent years have been necessary.

I am optimistic and excited about the future under our new manager, Brendan Rodgers. I have spoken to him about his plans and what he has said has been very impressive. He is someone who is enthusiastic about football and he lives and breathes it 24/7. He is very knowledgeable about tactics and he is determined to get Liverpool punching its weight again. Those are good qualities to have. I am eager to play for him and I think that, even though I am 32, he is a manager who can make me a better player.

I have always taken the view in my career that I will try to learn from the new people I come across, whether that be team-mates or managers. No matter how much I have won in my career, and even though I am approaching my 600th game for the club this season, I know there are things I can do better. And I am sure, listening to Brendan's ideas for how the game should be played, that I can continue to push myself in a red shirt.

But it isn't about what is good for me, it is what is best for Liverpool Football Club. That has always been the case in my eyes and always will continue to be.

Here's to a successful season.

CAREER STATISTICS

By Ged Rea and Dave Ball, official LFC statisticians.
(Up to and including 2011-12 season)

VITAL STATISTICS

Name	Steven Gerrard
D.O.B	30 May, 1980
Height	1.83m
Weight	83 kg
Boot Size	9

LIVERPOOL FC DEBUT

29 November 1998
F.A. Premier League
Liverpool 2 Blackburn Rovers 0
Att: 41,753
Ref: Mr J. Winter (Cleveland)
Scorers:
Ince 30, Owen 33.

Liverpool:
David James; Vegard Heggem (Steven Gerrard, 90),
Jamie Carragher, Steve Staunton (Bjorn Tore Kvarme, 75),
Phil Babb, Stig Inge Bjornebye; Jamie Redknapp,
Paul Ince, Patrik Berger; Robbie Fowler, Michael Owen.
Unused subs: Brad Friedel, Danny Murphy,
David Thompson.

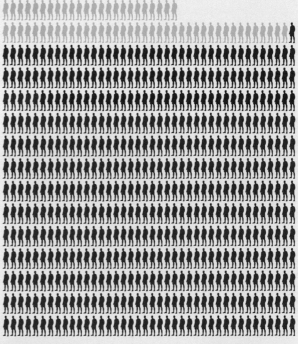

APPEARANCES

League	405
Europe	116
Other	63
TOTAL	584

LIVERPOOL F.C. RECORD APPEARANCES

at end of May 2012

LEAGUE
1.	Ian Callaghan	640
2.	Billy Liddell	492
3.	Jamie Carragher	484
4.	Emlyn Hughes	474
5.	Ray Clemence	470
6.	Ian Rush	469
7.	Tommy Smith	467
8.	Phil Neal	455
9.	Bruce Grobbelaar	440
13.	Steven Gerrard	405

EUROPE
1.	Jamie Carragher	139
2.	Steven Gerrard	116
3.	Sami Hyypia	94
4.	Ian Callaghan	89
5.	Tommy Smith	85
6.	Ray Clemence	80
7.	Emlyn Hughes	79
8.	John Arne Riise	79
9.	Jose Reina	76
10.	Phil Neal	74

OVERALL
1.	Ian Callaghan	857
2.	Jamie Carragher	699
3.	Ray Clemence	665
4.	Emlyn Hughes	665
5.	Ian Rush	660
6.	Phil Neal	650
7.	Tommy Smith	638
8.	Bruce Grobbelaar	628
9.	Alan Hansen	620
10.	Steven Gerrard	584

2001 2003 2005

LIVERPOOL HONOURS (winners' medals)

League Cup 2001, 2003, 2012
F.A.Cup 2001, 2006
UEFA Cup 2001
European Super Cup 2001
UEFA Champions League 2005

Steven was born on 30 May, 1980 – 24 days after Liverpool brought down the curtain on their 12th League title-winning campaign.

He has scored 38 goals for Liverpool in Europe, the most by any British player in the history of European competition.

Steven has netted 149 goals for the Reds in all competitions – his first was scored past Sheffield Wednesday 'keeper Kevin Pressman in a 4-1 win in December 1999.

He was the first Liverpool player to score under the managership of Rafa Benitez – doing so in a Champions League qualifier in Graz in August 2004.

When scoring against Arsenal in the Champions League in April 2008 Steven became the first Liverpool player to score in four successive European games at Anfield.

The Reds' skipper lies 10th in the club's all-time appearances list with 584. The player immediately above him is Alan Hansen who played 620 games.

INDIVIDUAL HONOURS

PFA Young Player of the Year 2001
PFA Player of the Year 2006
FWA Footballer of the Year 2009

He has won more International caps while with Liverpool than any other British-born Reds player – 96 for England.

Steven has scored five hat-tricks for his club – against Aston Villa and Everton in the league, Luton Town in the F.A. Cup and Total Network Solutions and Napoli in Europe.

The club he has scored most often against in a Liverpool shirt is Aston Villa – 10 of his goals have come against the Midlanders.

Steven was voted Man of the Match in both the 2005 Champions League Final and the F.A. Cup Final 12 months later.

He has captained Liverpool on more occasions in the Premier League than any other player – 249 times with a win ratio of 51%. In total he has been skipper in 354 Reds games.

Steven was awarded an MBE in the 2007 New Year Honours List.

SEASON	LEAGUE		F.A.CUP		LEAGUE CUP	
	APPS	GLS	APPS	GLS	APPS	GLS
1998–1999	4 + (8)	0	0	0	0	0
1999–2000	26 + (3)	1	2	0	0	0
2000–2001	29 + (4)	7	2 + (2)	1	4	0
2001–2002	26 + (2)	3	2	0	0	0
2002–2003	32 + (2)	5	2	0	6	2
2003–2004	34	4	3	0	1 + (1)	0
2004–2005	28 + (2)	7	0	0	3	2
2005–2006	32	10	6	4	1	1
2006–2007	35 + (1)	7	1	0	1	1
2007–2008	32 + (2)	11	1 + (2)	3	1 + (1)	1
2008–2009	30 + (1)	16	3	1	0	0
2009–2010	32 + (1)	9	2	1	0 + (1)	0
2010–2011	20 + (1)	4	1	0	0	0
2011–2012	12 + (6)	5	6	2	3 + (1)	2
Total	372 + (33)	89	31 + (4)	12	20 + (4)	9

(up to end of 2011-12 season) Appearances are listed as starts with substitute appearances in brackets.

2006   2007   2008   2009   2010   2011   2012   2013

Steven became the second youngest captain to lift the European Cup when the Reds won the trophy in 2005.

He was appointed Liverpool's club captain in October 2003 in succession to Sami Hyypia.

When scoring in the 2006 F.A. Cup Final, Steven became the first man ever to score in the finals of the F.A. Cup, League Cup, UEFA Cup and Champions League.

He captained England in Fabio Capello's first game in charge in February 2008.

Steven is the last Liverpool player to be voted PFA Young Player of the Year, winning the award in 2001.

He started his Liverpool career wearing the number 28 shirt before switching to number 17 and eventually number 8 in 2004 following the sale of Emile Heskey.

Steven has been named in the PFA Premier League Team of the Year on seven occasions – 2001 and each year from 2004 to 2009.

He scored 28 goals in 248 games under Gerard Houllier and 104 in 292 while Rafa Benitez was manager.

In the 2006 World Cup Finals in Germany he was England's leading scorer with two goals, while four years later in South Africa he was one of only three players to find the net for his country.

His most productive season for Liverpool in terms of goals was the 2008-09 season when he scored 24 times.

Against Kaunas in August 2005 Steven Gerrard became the first player in Liverpool history to score in five successive games in Europe.

He scored twice in his 100th appearance in Europe for the Reds in the unforgettable 4-0 home win over Real Madrid in March 2009.

His 149 goals have been scored against 83 different goalkeepers including five who at one time have played for the Reds – David James, Brad Friedel, Paul Jones, Brad Jones and Chris Kirkland.

Steven has scored a hat-trick for Liverpool in League, F.A. Cup, League Cup and European football. Only Ian Rush has achieved the feat in four or more different competitions for the club.

86 of his goals have been scored in front of his home crowd with 63 coming away from Anfield.

On 6 November 2002 Steven captained Liverpool for the first time in a 3-1 League Cup victory over Southampton at Anfield.

EUROPE		WORLD CLUB		F.A. COMM SHIELD		TOTAL	
APPS	GLS	APPS	GLS	APPS	GLS	APPS	GLS
1	0	0	0	0	0	5 + (8)	0
0	0	0	0	0	0	28 + (3)	1
9	2	0	0	0	0	44 + (6)	10
14 + (1)	1	0	0	0	0	42 + (3)	4
11	0	0	0	1	0	52 + (2)	7
7 + (1)	2	0	0	0	0	45 + (2)	6
10	4	0	0	0	0	41 + (2)	13
8 + (4)	7	2	1	0	0	49 + (4)	23
10 + (2)	3	0	0	0 + (1)	0	47 + (4)	11
13	6	0	0	0	0	47 + (5)	21
8 + (2)	7	0	0	0	0	41 + (3)	24
13	2	0	0	0	0	47 + (2)	12
1 + (1)	4	0	0	0	0	22 + (2)	8
0	0	0	0	0	0	21 + (7)	9
105 + (11)	38	2	1	1 + (1)	0	531 + (53)	149

Total   584   149

GOALS

42
38
34
31
30
28

Thierry Henry AFC
Steven Gerrard LFC
Ruud van Nistelrooy MUFC
Didier Drogba CFC
Wayne Rooney MUFC
Ryan Giggs MUFC
Peter Lorimer LUFC
Denis Law MUFC
Alan Shearer NUFC

MOST GOALS IN EUROPE FOR ONE ENGLISH CLUB (Up to and including 2011-12 season)

LIVERPOOL F.C. GOALSCORERS
(all competitions)
at end of 2011/2012 season

Ian Rush	346
Roger Hunt	286
Gordon Hodgson	241
Billy Liddell	228
Robbie Fowler	183
Kenny Dalglish	172
Michael Owen	158
Harry Chambers	151
Steven Gerrard	149
Sam Raybould	129
Jack Parkinson	128
Dick Forshaw	124

WHEN STEVEN'S 149 GOALS HAVE COME

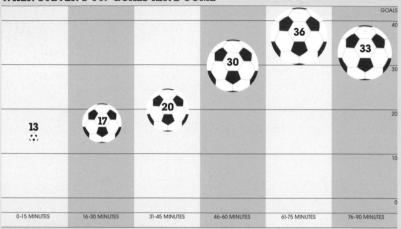

GOALS
40
30
20
10
0

13
17
20
30
36
33

0-15 MINUTES | 16-30 MINUTES | 31-45 MINUTES | 46-60 MINUTES | 61-75 MINUTES | 76-90 MINUTES

STEVEN GERRARD'S LIVERPOOL GOALS at end of 2011/2012 season

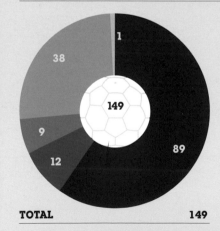

149

1
38
9
12
89

TOTAL	149
League	89
F.A. Cup	12
League Cup	9
Europe	38
World Club Champs	1

League   89

9 - Aston Villa
7 - Bolton W., Everton, Newcastle U.
6 - Birmingham C.
5 - Manchester U., West Ham U.
4 - Blackburn R., Middlesbrough
3 - Arsenal, Hull C., Manchester C.,
    Sunderland, West Bromwich A.
2 - Burnley, Charlton A., Fulham,
    Leeds U., Portsmouth,
    Tottenham H.
1 - Chelsea, Coventry C., Derby Co.,
    Reading, Sheffield U., Sheffield W.,
    Southampton, Wolverhampton W.

F.A. Cup   12

3 - Luton T.
2 - West Ham U.
1 - Brighton & H.A., Everton, Luton T.,
    Oldham A., Portsmouth,
    Reading, Tranmere R.

League Cup   9

2 - Manchester C., Watford
1 - Arsenal, Aston Villa, Cardiff C.,
    C. Palace, Manchester U.

Europe   38

5 - Total Network Solutions
4 - Marseille
3 - Napoli, PSV Eindhoven
2 - Besiktas, AK Graz, FBK Kaunas,
    Levski Sofia, Olympiakos,
    Real Madrid
1 - AC Milan, Alaves, Arsenal, Atletico
    Madrid, Bordeaux, Dynamo Kiev,
    Inter Milan, Lille, Porto, Rabotnicki,
    Unirea Urziceni

World Club Champs   1

1 - Deportivo Saprissa